I crossed paths with Samantha when my work as an Eco-theologian and her involvement with ecovillage and sustainability activism met. Her altruism for people and the planet touched me deeply. After her son was born, I saw her enter a path of deep soul work, something she hadn't given much time to. She came out of a rocky journey smelling like a rose. This book shares her touching story.

—*Michael Dowd, bestselling author, eco-theologian. Ypsilanti, Michigan*

Samantha Song's story made me laugh, cry, inquire and reflect on how fortunate I am to know both her and her children. It is impressive how Samantha navigates life-altering decisions with timely perseverance. Her story is a treasure to behold; a reminder that we're all in this together and that it takes commitment and ingenuity to follow one's heart. This book clearly defines her walk through life as a compassionate and generous mother, daughter, sibling, co-worker, friend, and ally.

—*Grace Collins, entrepreneur, author, teacher. New Orleans, Louisiana.*

I was swept up by this story. The real and raw emotions revealed speak to the depth of the female experience of embodiment and bonding. It's a story of finding your way amidst confusing life choices—following your heart and your inner voice even in the face of disappointing others. I was inspired by Samantha's vulnerability and authenticity.

—*Corinna Wood, holistic healing teacher. Black Mountain, NC.*

Samantha's insightful journey involves all aspects and intricacies of the adoption triad. As an adoptee myself, I was touched by the heartfelt vulnerability of the author. Kudos for a remarkable book.
—*Valerie Naiman, ecovillage founder, author of* Mystic Masquerade, an Adoptee's Search for Truth. *Platteville, Costa Rica.*

Hey you beautiful people! I know this story like the back of my hand. I have loved being a friend, witness, and of mutual support to this adventurous soul. Mentoring Samantha's son in the aftermath of the rugged landing he had on this planet has been an honor. What an awesome and memorable read.
—*Tree Malpass, teacher, storyteller, philosopher, wilderness guide, mechanic, handyman, traveler, mentor. Tybee Island, Georgia.*

Samantha opens her heart and shares her story as if speaking with a trusted friend walking through life together. It is a journey driven by fearless independence, innocence, loyalties, and courage. Adventures cropped up where I was taken aback, and then where I cheered them on. And for the first time, a light was shone on my own heartache, to an understanding from when my mother and I also went through a long separation shortly after my birth, ours due to her illness. I now imagined how difficult this must have been for my mother, not just me. My heart softened with a new and broader compassion.
—*Penny Tourville, teacher, woman of faith. St. Paul, Minnesota.*

As a child I was selfishly taken from my biological mother and given no choice but to believe it was safer for me to live with what was an inadequate replacement. When I became a mother, I experienced the mother-daughter bond, but a tumultuous divorce separated me from my daughter. This book has been instrumental in helping me recognize how fabricated lies had me believe it was better that my child was without me, that I needed to protect her from me, and helped me instead recognize my truth and restart my journey back to restoring what was severed.
—*Marissa Leigh, physician assistant, human rights advocate. NY, NY.*

I was left speechless with the articulate sharing of Samantha's life's journey. Even though I knew her adoption story, I could not close the book. I was overwhelmed with the raw emotion shared from the depths of her heart's pain and joy. She touched me with her transparency in sharing some of her most vulnerable and intimate life's emotions, frailties and unmitigated courage.
—*Shanti Plett, entrepreneur, ASL interpreter. Winnipeg, Canada.*

To Peg —

You've heard some stories about my fun adventures, and some not so fun adventures! But it all turned out okay. Enjoy filling in some of the gaps of my wild ride. Thanks for our longtime friendship!

Samantha Song
aka Jill

Giving Birth to an Empty Nest

A Mother's Journey of Adoption, Revocation, and Healing

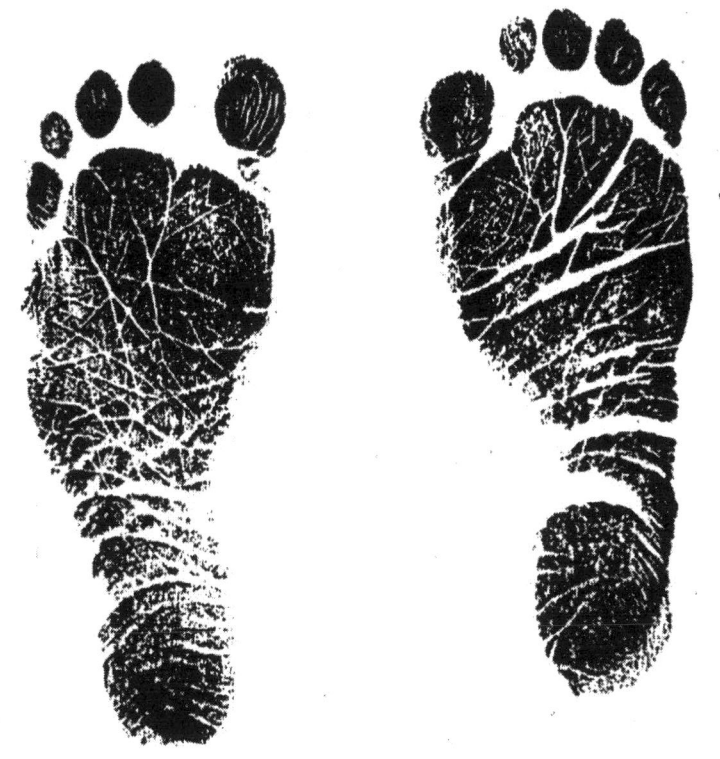

Samantha Song

Shanti Publishing, USA

Copyright © 2023 by Samantha Song
No part of this book may be reproduced in any manner without permission in writing from the author: samanthasong2020@gmail.com

Formatting and Editing by Ramajon
Cover and Typographic Design by Pepi Acebo
Cover Photo by Siede Preis/Photodisc/Getty Images
Illustrations by Aziza Archer, Kyra Peregrine, Lynn Song, and Spencer Elbert

This novel is wrapped in sacred cloth, containing a blend of imagined characters and incidents. I gathered ideas for this writing from observations, reading, and life experiences. Then I put that recipe in a blender and drank the mysterious potion. I survived the subsequent drunken turbulent journey and was further impelled to spin this tale of magical outcomes. Except for portrayals of myself written in whimsical ways, resemblance to actual persons, locales, and anecdotes, is coincidental. We all ride the waves of life's escapades playing various roles. What I do know is whatever was in that concoction, I've been drunk on life ever since.

Book ISBN: 979-8-9886451-0-8
eBook ISBN: 979-8-9886451-1-5
audiobook ISBN: 979-8-988651-2-2

Shanti Publishing™

Printed in USA on recycled acid free paper.

*Dedicated to
my parents, Eve and Bernard,*

my son, Lynn,

*and to Nancy Verrier for teaching
me what I needed to know to
preserve my motherhood.*

Contents

A Glimpse at the Main Characters xvi
   Mother/Family xvi
   Birth Team xvi
   Baby Em's Names xvii
   Other Characters xvii
   Maine Hometown Friends xvii
   Shenandoah Friends xvii
Foreword xviii
Prologue xx

Part I: Winter 1996 – Spring 1997 1
   1 Baby Em 3
      My Reasons for Circumventing Motherhood 4
      Family Reactions 5
      The Offer 7
      Let's Try Again 9
      Where to Live 10
      Baby Shower 11
      The Birth Team Gathers 12
      Blessings to Em 16
      Belly Cast 17
      Get Some Sleep 18
   2 Giving Birth to an Empty Nest 21
      Off to the Hospital 22
      Ready Or Not, Here He Comes! 23

Welcome to the World 25
All Alone with My Grief 26
3 KIDNAPPED 28
Hospital Ward with My Newborn 28
Visitors 29
Buying Time from the Inevitable 30
Sticking with "Best Laid Plans" 32
Severing the Bond 34
Separation Trauma 35
Lingering Discomfort 37
Signing Adoption Papers 39
Easier Said Than Done 39
Turning the Tide 41
4 HELL'S ROLLER COASTER 44
Guilt and Maternal Instinct Duking It Out 45
Please Take Him Back 46
Teeter Totter 47
Birthmother Outcry 49
Tick Tock Tick Tock 50
The Storm 51
Defeated 53
Denial 54
5 ADOPTEES, BIRTHMOTHERS, AND ADOPTIVE PARENTS 56
Valuable Insight 57
I Need to See a Lawyer 59
6 FOUR-LEAF CLOVERS 60
Follow Up with Nancy 60
Seeing Lynn Again 62
Where is My Copy of the Adoption Papers? 64
Do I Have Any Legal Recourse? 65

  Pastor Harry, Can You Help Me? *66*
  Preparing a Nest *67*
  Telling Angela the Hard Truth *68*
  Homecoming! *69*
 7 IS THERE A LIGHT AT THE END OF THE TUNNEL? 71
  Atypical Parenting Initiation *71*
  Healing the Severed Bond *74*
  Postpartum Malaise on Steroids *75*
  Blessing Way *76*
  My Lifeline: Family and Friends *78*
  Cures for the Baby Blues *79*
  One Day at a Time *80*
  I'll Adopt You Both *81*
  I'll Quit Smoking If You Come Home *83*
  Infant Toddler Sign Language *85*
  Dark Night of the Soul, Ad Nauseam *85*
 8 DO YOU BELIEVE IN MIRACLES? 89
  Suicidal Ideation *90*
  Abracadabra! *92*
  Welcome Back! *93*
 9 CLEANING UP TRAIN WRECKS 96
  Making Ends Meet *96*
  Family Constellations *97*
  Facing Angela *97*
  We Love You All! *100*
  Everything is Possible for Samantha and Lynn *100*

PART II: FALL 1963 – WINTER 1996 103
 10 ADOPT THEM ALL 105
  Catholic School Sex Ed *105*

   My Parents *107*
   The Baby of the Family *109*
   Chores *110*
   Farm Excursions *111*
   Winter Fun *112*
   The Paper Route *112*
   Volunteer Work *113*
   Lost in the Shuffle *114*
   Abuse *116*
   High School Employment *117*
   My First Romance *117*
   Theatre *119*
   Being the Butt End of Jokes *120*
   The Travel Bug *121*

11 FREEDOM *122*
   Nursing Assistant Job *124*
   Changing College Majors *125*
   Not the Marrying Kind *126*

12 LEARNING CURVES *130*
   Adding Deaf Studies to My Curriculum *131*
   Graduate School *133*
   Internship in Belize *135*
   Hitching a Ride *136*
   A Budding Romance *137*
   Rustic Living *138*
   Tragedy Back at Home *139*
   Fierce Independence *141*

13 LOOKING FOR SHANGRI-LA *143*
   Feeling at Home with Relatives *144*
   Footloose and Fancy Free *146*

Home is Calling Me Back *147*
Hitchhiking.. *148*
Tragedy Hits Again *152*
Plan B... *153*

14 SUSTAINABLE LIVING, HERE AND ABROAD 156
The Final Frontier?.. *157*
Building a Cabin *160*
Finding My Niche *161*
Return to Belize.. *162*

15 DETOURS 165
Friends in Town.. *165*
Circling Back to the Baby Offer....................................... *166*
Heartthrobs *167*
Choosing a Sperm Donor... *168*
Tying Up Loose Ends *169*
Solidifying My Birth Team Support *169*

16 THE CONTRACT AND CREATING LIFE 172
If Only I Had Known *173*
Ignoring the Signs.. *174*
Fertile Murtle.. *175*
Miscarriage *175*
Travel as Salve *176*
The Dream *177*
Pregnancy *178*
Moving into Town *180*
Baby Em... *180*

PART III: SUMMER 1997 – SUMMER 2003 183

17 KIDS DO AND SAY THE FUNNIEST THINGS 185
Sleeping In... *185*

Mommy Mix-Up 186
Pure Fun! 187
School 189
Housemates 189
Cabin Life 190
Family Reunions 192
I Need to Talk to Peter Pan 192
The Art Car is Born 193
Sock Monkey Haven 196
Grandpa's Death 198
Growing Wings? 201

18 THANK YOU, BELIZE 202
Passports Trigger Longing 203
Flooded with Memories 204
Deaf Education 205
Orphanage 206
Reunions in the Village 207
Tropical Playground 209
Farewell My Friends, Have a Good Life 210

19 REUNIONS 212
June, Aka Jeong Sik Ko 213
Vanna's Long Search 216
Resolution for Harry 218
Crystal 219

20 SAVE THE GORILLAS 220
Letting Love Flow 224
Will You Commit Your Love? 226
Prize Fish 227
Not Saying Good-Bye This Time 229

21 REFLECTIONS 232

22 Twins!	237
Epilogue	239
Acknowledgments	244
My Inspiration	248
Books	*248*
Movies	*251*
Websites	*251*
About the Author	252

A Glimpse at the Main Characters

Mother/Family

MOTHER, SAMANTHA SONG: "Hi! Welcome, and watch me try to circumvent maternal instinct."

SAMANTHA'S PARENTS AND 15 SIBLINGS: "Tsk, tsk, tsk. Why can't you be normal?"

Birth Team

MIDWIFE, SAGE: "Push! I know you are tired, honey, but he's almost here."

ADOPTIVE MOTHER, ANGELA: "Thank you, Samantha and Ralph for gifting me this baby!"

BIOLOGICAL FATHER, RALPH: "Em, you have my grandfather's face. Way to go, DNA."

BIRTH COACH/BOYFRIEND, PETER (PAN): "Welcome little one! When you are old enough to eat solids, I'll bring you healthy foods made from seeds and sunshine."

FRIENDS, LIAM: "Cardinals are your birds; Serviceberry is your tree."

CHRISTINE: "You are a star!"

VANNA*: "Will someone tell me where my mother is? I haven't seen her in 50 years."

Baby Em's Names

FIRST BIRTH CERTIFICATE: Em Lynn Pan Song

ADOPTIVE NAME: Lynn Manning

NEW NAME ON BIRTH CERTIFICATE: Lynn Liam Song

Other Characters

VANNA'S SOCK MONKEY, GEORGE

VANNA'S SEARCH ANGEL, MARY: "I'll find her."

PASTOR, HARRY: "Let's go for a hike. You need to get outside!"

COUNSELOR, NANCY VERRIER: "I understand your loss, Samantha. You are bonded with your baby."

Maine Hometown Friends

JUNE (JEONG)*: "I'm sorry. Please forgive me. Thank you. I love you."

DAVE: "You'll change your mind."

Shenandoah Friends

CHAZ: "What am I going to tell my mother about you?!"

PHYLLIS: "Learn to meditate. It can save you."

BRIAN: "I'll teach Lynn sign language."

CRYSTAL*: "Lynn, I want to call you my brother."

SPENCER: "Samantha I decided I'll go with you."

* ADOPTEES: June, Crystal, Vanna

Foreword

HAVING HELPED REAR HER YOUNGER siblings when she was still a child herself, Samantha Song was sure that she never wanted to have children of her own. However, when a friend wanted but couldn't bear children, she decided that it would be a great gift to bear a child for her. Meticulously making a list of agreements, including allowing Samantha and the "sperm donor" to take part in the child's life, and surrounding herself with a wonderful group of people to help with the birth and relinquishment; everything seemed foolproof. However, when the baby was born, Samantha was struck by the intensity of her love for her baby and began to realize that giving her baby away was something she couldn't do.

This is the story of the struggle between Samantha's mind-felt obligation to her friend and her heart-felt longing for her baby, which ultimately resulted in the baby's being returned to her. One of the truly amazing parts of this story is how mature and fair all the adults were when this happened. Although the adoptive mother was, of course, upset and saddened by having to return the baby, she eventually agreed to talk things over. Their friendship was renewed and, as time progressed, they each had children who became friends.

It is very important for adults to remember the power of the mother/child relationship. The experience in the womb has a tremendous impact on both mother and child, and although the mother may miss her baby, this doesn't compare to how traumatic the disappearance of the mother is on the child. We may fail to realize or forget that children know who their mothers are, but babies, through their implicit sensory memory, do not forget.

—*Nancy Verrier, LMFT, author, lecturer, and mother. Author of* The Primal Wound: Understanding the Adopted Child *and* Coming Home to Self: The Adopted Child Grows Up.

Prologue

IT TOOK A SPECIAL HIDDEN CALLING mixed with high drama to transform my conviction about never wanting to have a child. This story is my journey out of that matrix. While in the throes of living on the edge of insufferable emotional pain, I was transformed by a series of interventions that birthed the homecoming of my spirit. Embracing the moment, welcoming the flow, and learning to trust the bigger picture, even if unknown, are lessons that came out of hiding. Rumi's[1] poem alludes to the wisdom of learning to expect the unexpected:

> *Who makes these changes?*
> *I shoot an arrow right.*
> *It lands left.*
> *I ride after a deer and find myself*
> *Chased by a hog.*
> *I plot to get what I want*
> *And end up in prison.*
> *I dig pits to trap others*
> *And fall in.*
> *I should be suspicious*
> *Of what I want.*

---

[1] Rumi translations in this book are by Coleman Barks, unless otherwise noted. Permission given for usage therein.

In Part I, I share my biggest "assignment" in this school of life: the time period of my son Lynn's first year of living in this world. This first section includes the work of cleaning up a train wreck; from something that began as a creative adventure and ended up with me navigating an enormous blind curve. In Part II, I share a summary of my life and what my survival mechanism dialed into: making the most of life, sometimes without foresight, but always with lessons to learn. Finally, in Part III, I share the light I found at the end of the tunnel. The holy universe always had my back, even though this was not obvious when passing through dark passageways. Hindsight is 2020.

Hopefully my reunion with Lynn and giving him lots of affection over time was balm enough to provide healing for the early trauma, even when remnants of it echo into the present to be further healed. At least we had not been separated for what could have been a lifetime!

May my story provide insight to those who offer to become surrogate moms, those who are planning to relinquish their babies for adoption, adoptive parents, and for adoptees. May it also be an inspiration for whatever your life's challenges are. As we know, they come in an infinite variety of packages. When life's lessons become tumultuous journeys, may you find the strength to do what it takes to hang in there, leaving enough room for surprise, miracles and hope to blossom.

—*Samantha Song, Earth Day 2023*

Part I
Winter 1996 – Spring 1997

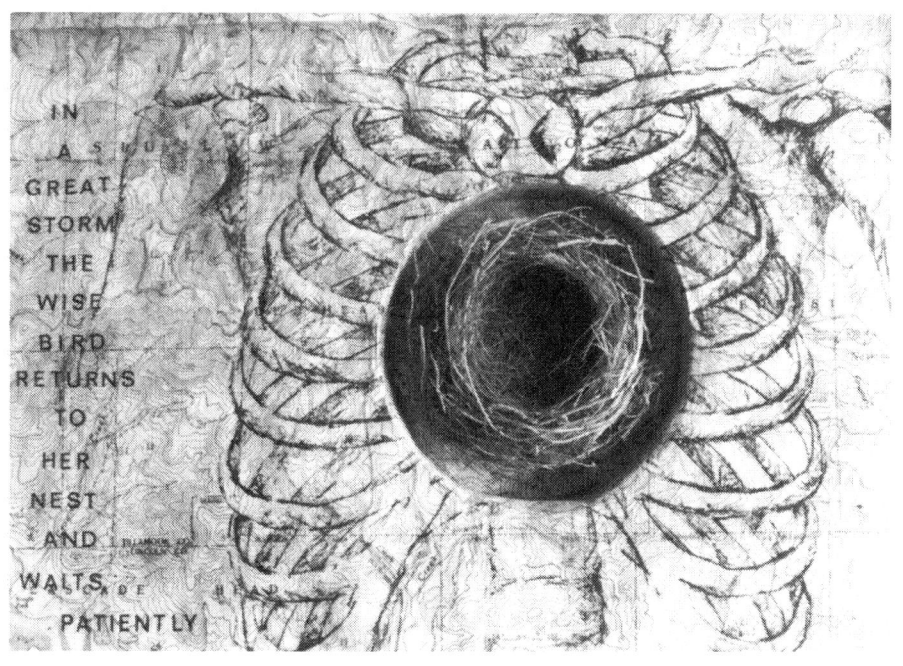

Aziza Archer, artist

1
Baby Em

My heart was pounding as I dialed the number. "Ring-a-ling-a-ling," reverberated through the phone. I was feeling a mixture of excitement and sadness as I faced the fear of talking to my mother. I had been through this scenario before when my first pregnancy ended in a miscarriage. "Ring-a-ling-a-ling."

"Hello?"

"Hi, Mom. Are you sitting down?"

"Samantha?"

"Yes, I have some big news that I've been afraid to tell you."

Silence.

"Mom?"

"Yes? Oh no! Now what, honey? I am sitting down, and I am listening."

"Thanks, Mom. I'm sitting down too, wrapped in the lovely quilt you hand-stitched for me when I moved away." I said in the best cheery voice I could garner. "OK, umm… remember I have been trying to have a baby for my friend?" Then I blurted it out. "I need to tell you that I'm eight months pregnant. It's a boy."

"What?! Pregnant for your friend again?!" She gasped.

"Please listen. I wasn't going to tell you this time."

"Oh, Samantha, you are so full of surprises. What can I say? Congratulations? You could bring the baby home and your family will take care of him. You know your brother Scott and his wife have had trouble conceiving and are talking about adopting.

What about them? It's family," she cried. "When are you going to settle down? You're making me old bef—"

"Stop! I didn't want to tell you because I was upset about the way you handled my miscarriage last year, and if I told you, then everyone would find out. And they would all talk down to me again. I'm sorry. Forgive me, please?"

"Samantha, I will try to forgive you, but I need some time, and are you sure?" Her voice cracked.

"I'm 33 years old, Mom. Don't you think I know what I am doing? And anyway, it's too late to go back on my word. Tell Dad for me, will you?"

"OK. I'd better let you go. I need some time to think and pray. Let's talk later. I love you," she said in a tearful voice.

"Thanks Mom. I love you too. Bye."

"Click." She had ended the conversation quickly.

I too had been in a hurry to get this call over with. Lowering the handset to my heart I held it as though I was holding tightly onto my mother's hand. I rocked myself, crying. When I could unclench my fingers, I laid the slobbery wet phone down. My mother was hurt, and I certainly didn't want to hurt her. I was already feeling a need to brace myself as the birth approached but was adamant about following the agreement I had made. Sitting in my cozy cabin on a love seat, hugging myself, I reviewed in my mind what had led up to this position I found myself in.

My Reasons for Circumventing Motherhood

My heart had gone out to my friend, Angela, who physically could not bear children, when I offered this most precious gift. I didn't realize that other people might not see this as a blessing. Fit, strong, and assumedly fertile, I saw I could give a child a life and—

to a woman who had an extensive life-long network and a neighborhood full of connections—someone she could love, imagining that lucky child would have a good home and vibrant support with capable and loving people.

The mainstay of my life was full of projects and adventures, some that included extensive travel, to consider raising a family. Embarking on this journey would give me an opportunity to experience pregnancy and birthing, and be extended family to this child.

This vision included committing to be a back-up person, taking on motherhood if something happened to the adoptive mother. We assumed, in our fabricated story, that this would not be needed. It never occurred to me that offering something so sacred might not be the brightest idea. With only a month to go, I was beginning to realize that messing with Mother Nature is risky at best and knew I had to be strong for a little while longer.

Because of what I knew of the enormous caretaking responsibilities of parenting, from seeing my mom juggle raising 16 kids, with us older ones helping to care for the younger ones, I was able to continue to rationalize my stance, and now, my plan. In this scenario there was an escape from years of motherhood duties. I'd had my fill of caring for younger siblings for years. Having "been there, and done that," I was planning on continuing to enjoy my freedom.

Family Reactions

The news of a *second* unconventional pregnancy spread like wildfire through my family grapevine. They weren't swallowing it. Maybe I should have kept my mouth shut. Instead, after attending a personal growth workshop about radical honesty, where tips were taught on living an honest, transparent life, I'd decided to share about the pending arrival. Although I might have pulled off keeping it under wraps, I just didn't want to be holding such a big, special secret from them. My "famn damily" had plenty of time for this odd choice of mine to have sunk in from the same scenario a year earlier, except this time I was about to deliver.

As I'd half expected, in the next week I received phone calls and letters mostly voicing strong opinions against my choice. Many of them spewed the same bile as the last time. My sister Margaret even told me she would never speak to me again. Nonetheless, I had faced my fear of what their reactions might cause and instead embraced the belief that I knew what I was doing. I hoped it would demonstrate a new perspective on how families are formed; something they could eventually accept and maybe appreciate.

On a sunny morning while pondering the unwelcome feedback, as I walked over to my kitchenette to make a cup of tea, I couldn't help being aware of some of the ways that my sweet plan might have gone sour. Passing a mirror, I caught a glimpse of myself and stopped. I made myself stand tall and look proud, my blue eyes staring back at me, and then winked at myself as if with approval. My long auburn braids outlined my engorged breasts and basketball-shaped belly bursting from underneath my farmer's pants. I gave myself a thumbs up. After pouring myself some tea, I waddled back to the love seat and slowly sat down. Then I ripped up all the nasty letters I had received.

I had been hoping for support and sympathy when I told my family. Hadn't they had friends who wanted to have a child, but couldn't without adopting? Could they not imagine how difficult and expensive adoption is? My thoughts were racing. I wondered what they knew about birthmothers who relinquish their babies under varying circumstances. Did they ever know anyone who was adopted?

My baby was going to a good home. What had I forgotten to consider? It was a little late to ask where the template was for this complex arrangement. My naivete was becoming self-evident.

Two and a half weeks before my due date, I was further disappointed to learn that my sister Sue and her husband, who lived back in my hometown 1000 miles away, had passed by within 20 miles of me without stopping to visit; Ouch! They were on their way home from Mardi Gras festivities in New Orleans, planning to surprise me, when they heard the news. Sue's husband wouldn't even let her call me. What did he know that I didn't? What I knew was that most of my 15 siblings were ashamed of me, some more vocally than others. I remembered that my mother, trying to be supportive and stay neutral, had said it was ultimately my choice. I actually knew, along with being reinforced by my siblings, that deep inside, she felt sad and disappointed. A part of me was feeling torn between my family's reactions and the commitment I had made to Angela.

In sharing my secret with my mother, which was like sharing it with the world, I had once again opened myself up to the questioning and judgements of others, so it was important to stay strong in my conviction. I needed to resist succumbing to others' influences and wishes, whether for me or themselves. I was beginning to understand what was meant by "no good deed goes unpunished." But just what was wrong with my altruistic offer? Why couldn't my family see I was giving the greatest gift possible? I tried to shake off the negative commentary, quell my wavering thoughts, and dug my heels in to keep my composure despite it all.

The Offer

The arrangement had started out rather innocently. My friend, Angela, whom I had met when I was new to the area, had been looking to adopt a newborn. With so many parents in line to do the same, the adoption agencies were giving married couples preference for this. When we met, Angela was 31, like me. Both of us were from a Catholic upbringing and single. We were volunteering on the same weekly shift at the local food co-op and had lots of time working alongside each other to get to know one another. Angela wanted to start a family with a clean slate. I had listened to her talk a lot about this topic, sharing her sadness around her dream as it was beginning to shatter. From that, I started to imagine a win-win outcome, without giving it a lot of deep thought or study, but it was heavy on my mind.

One sunny afternoon, after hiking up to the top of a glorious 360-degree mountain view, we were standing amidst a heavenly backdrop and catching our breath when I blurted out, "Hey Angela, remember what I told you about my mom? She popped out 16 kids. Well, I don't think I want to take care of another rug rat, maybe that sounds crass, but I got pretty burned out on all the responsibility of being an older child. I've been thinking about offering to have a baby for you; someone who longs for that experience."

She looked stunned. "Really?" she asked, squinting at me in disbelief, and then taking a deep breath.

I wiped the sweat off my forehead and took a sip of cold mountain water, feeling a strange sense of adrenaline run through me, and nodded enthusiastically as I looked at her intently. "Really," I said. "It might be great to experience the miraculous pregnancy part, but with my life already so busy, I don't think I could handle the full-time aftermath. I could do with being a special auntie, though."

After another minute of stunned silence, Angela came closer and hugged me. She looked into my eyes as though to gauge my sincerity. I had her full attention. I said, "My best friend June, from my hometown, had a baby during her first year in college. She wasn't ready to be a mom without much support, and her son has a great family. She gets to see him about once a month." I was accustomed to making the most out of life and had taken plenty of risks. Why not this? "I know, we would have to find a donor, but I have lots of friends who would be willing candidates. Think about it. Let the idea sink in. We can talk next week."

We walked back down the mountain trail. The wind was lapping at our faces; two friends enjoying the evergreens, the budding trees, rock outcroppings, and the pink and white blossoms of spring.

There was a lot to think about and discuss; things could get tricky, but we jumped on this unique creative possibility with enthusiasm. Many conversations ensued and agreements were formulated. There would be no money involved; I would not *sell* my child. Ours would be a model story, unlike the controversial story from the 1980s about "Baby M," whose birthmother[2] fought bitterly in court to get custody of her biological child.

Let's Try Again

Fast forward. Three months into my first pregnancy, I had a miscarriage. The emotional pangs I felt from the loss gave me a hint that I was dealing with a deeper emotional connection than I had anticipated. Incidentally, my family and some friends were relieved of their concerns.

Six months later, in my cabin in the woods, I conceived again. Just as before, using artificial insemination, I got pregnant on the first try.

---

[2] From *Adoption Healing: a path to recovery* (2000) by Joe Soll: "The term 'birthmother' is used to describe a woman who has surrendered her child to adoption, not a woman who is pregnant."

We were more prepared the second time around. Things materialized quickly and smoothly. In looking back on memory lane, the early pre-pregnancy dialogues are a bit of a blur.

Soon I was having "Baby Em" (an affectionate name I had called him, short for "Embryo"). I imagined this time in my womb would probably be the closest I might feel to him.

Our plan was written in a way that included an exemplary open adoption with a written contract, separate from other legal papers. Open adoption involves agreements in which the biological and adoptive families are in contact with one another to varying degrees. It was my understanding that adopted children from these kinds of amicable relationships do well with the separation. Don't they?

For all I knew my child would not have abandonment issues. He would know the exemplary story of his birth into this world and would see that his biological parents still loved him, despite being away working. We believed we were making important contributions to society and would have a good influence on him. There would be an opportunity for him to have a relationship with us, plus our large extended families if he ever needed.

Where to Live

I had been keeping my eyes on a new townhouse project close to Angela's that was being built, with an anticipated completion date just before I was due. After inquiring about the units for sale, imagining multiple bonuses with having a place in town, I decided to buy in. Angela would need me those first several months supplying and delivering breast milk, and it would be more convenient to visit the baby. After that initial adjustment I would have the opportunity to take more work in town. My townhouse could be a resource for other ecovillage members living in our rural undeveloped setting (laundry machines and warm showers would be a luxury I could offer). And while traveling out of the country for extended periods or spending summers living in my rustic cabin, I could rent out the townhouse and use some of the proceeds to support a small school for deaf kids that I was planning to open in Belize.

The well-thought-out details, agreements and signed contracts were falling into place to provide support to all involved-or so we thought. I ignored any feelings that would interfere with my intentions to follow through with my idealistic plan. Covering my feelings was a big smile and a convincing attitude, I really didn't think anyone could know what I was doing better than me. Some marveled at my generosity. A perfect storm, but who knew?

By my last month of pregnancy, we were full of excitement and anticipation. I had chosen a group of six close friends to help me get moved and, more importantly, help me through the birthing process—all of them dynamic environmentalists who wanted to save the planet for future generations. Why not make it a party? These invited birth *doulas* and a seasoned midwife would be with me at the hospital during the delivery, where I would have medical back-up support if there were any complications.

Baby Shower

My friend Vanna hosted a celebratory baby shower at Angela's place. Vanna was a clay artist I had befriended at the ecovillage she helped start-where I had been living. Her sandy-red hair matched the color of the pottery she made, along with her clay-stained hands and fingernails. Even the plastered adobe home she lived in matched her hair. Besides being an innovative artist, she strongly identified herself as having been adopted and was keenly interested in witnessing this unusual event. To commemorate my pregnancy, she thought up an idea for the group to make a plaster casting of my bulged belly.

The day dawned brightly. Outside my cabin window the sunshine sparkled through new leaves waving on the trees. Stumbling up out of bed, feeling as big as an ox, I walked over and steadied myself then slowly sat down on the compost toilet and did my duty. Perched there, I gave myself a sponge bath. I struggled to slather on some coconut oil, especially on my dry legs. Soon my body would be mine again, all mine, no longer a vessel for this intimate stranger who was now kicking me awake at night. But I would miss him.

I refused to dwell on that part.

When I was all primped up, dressed in my favorite short-sleeved green cotton maternity dress, I carefully danced around the room as the comfy skirt billowed out, giving me plenty of room to move. I was ready to go when Vanna pulled up. I was happy for the ride because with my enormous belly; it was getting harder for me to maneuver myself behind the steering wheel of my car.

"Come on big mama, let's get you plastered," she said as she hooked her elbow through mine and escorted me to the passenger seat, helping me up into her terra cotta colored pickup.

The Birth Team Gathers

An hour later, while driving into Angela's neighborhood, we passed people working in a community garden that Angela had started. Spring peas were beginning to sprout. There were lots of kids hanging out with their families—either on a walk or playing at the kid-friendly park. We pulled up to Angela's stylish, brick-faced bungalow that was beautifully landscaped with pine trees and boxwoods. Daffodils were in bloom. We were greeted with hugs by the proud adopting mother. "Hi. Happy to see you two. How about some tea?"

"Do I smell chocolate?" I asked with a smile.

"Follow your nose. There are brownies in the kitchen. Is that baby hungry?" teased Angela. "And there's a nest for you in the living room."

Angela looked great with her fresh-cut short, brown curly hair, wearing wire-rimmed glasses, light makeup, dainty earrings, and a decorative scarf that gave her a smart sophisticated look with artsy flair. Soon she would have a mothers' glow.

Besides her volunteer job at the food co-op, and helping to tend a big garden, Angela was a Waldorf School teacher. I had seen how good she was with kids and had met her wide network of family, friends, neighbors, and colleagues. She had a "village" that would be of great support to her. I knew my son would have a great mom and a home knit into a community network just outside his front door. In our few years of friendship, I was mostly involved in the development of the rural ecovillage, but we had cultivated a deeper connection from her helping to orient me to the area and getting me out on scenic mountain hikes.

"Ralph, come in, and welcome." Angela shook hands with our son's biological father, who wasn't shy in the least about calling himself the "sperm donor." He had a distinctive handlebar mustache he was proud of, and prominent cheekbones. He was a member of our Community Supported Agriculture (CSA) farm at the ecovillage and a biology researcher working on the cutting edge of studies focused on the impact of greenhouse gases on the environment. With his impressive credentials, I had assumed he had good genes. He was a little hard to reach emotionally, and I was not attracted to him romantically—an important dynamic for a donor. Just the same, if something happened to Angela, he was committed to step in with me to take on a more active parenting role.

Peter, my birth-coach boyfriend, walked in with kombucha and a tray of carrots and celery sticks, kissing everyone on both cheeks. His vegetarian fare kept him on the thin side. I could wrap my arms around him, and then some. He taught NVC (nonviolent communication), managed the local food co-op, was a fantastic gardener and had fed me lots of healthy food throughout my pregnancy. Like me, Peter was from a large family and never wanted to have kids. My heart had gone out to him when I learned of a family tragedy he had endured. I sometimes called him Peter Pan, the lost boy. I got to love him, hold him tightly, and kiss his bruised heart.

Christine arrived next, in all her flamboyance; she was so much fun! She had a head full of blonde curls and looked like an adult Goldilocks, though she wasn't afraid of bears—Christine was not afraid of anyone. For someone of short stature, she sure commanded attention with her loud and confident voice. Her friendly and chill dog, a medium sized Chow/Akita mix named Beauregard Bonaparte Bocephus, Bodacious LaBarque ("Beau" for short), joined the party, content to hang out in the backyard where some of the day's rituals would be held. Christine was an aspiring actress with a background in theater, who had moved to the area with Peter, and another friend, Harry, all of them seeking to live in a smaller, hipster town with a milder climate, where they could share their skills. She had teamed up with me to organize bringing the National Theatre of the Deaf to perform *The King of Hearts* in town. We enjoyed the production process that culminated in a highly successful, sold-out event, and a fun friendship.

In the kitchen, while nibbling on the cornucopia of food on the table, I heard a train whistle come through the front door. Liam had arrived. He was a tall, handsome Native American man full of joy and celebration, a retired railroad engineer, and also a sailor, environmentalist, world traveler, and writer. He had moved a train caboose onto the ecovillage land and created the cutest tiny home not far from my cabin. His doorbell was a removable train whistle. If it wasn't hanging near his door, he wasn't home.

We would often sit by the fire at night, just outside his boxcar home, sharing our travel stories, then look up at the stars, making up new names for the constellations while splitting our guts in laughter as we tried to outdo each other's tales. He had a shadow side though, that would sometimes get the best of him. Among the hardest stories on his heart were family stories starting with the trauma of frequent early separations from his unstable mother. He realized this had undeniably had a negative impact on his adult relationships. There were also flashbacks that haunted him from his Vietnam days. I considered him a confidant and an elder brother.

As Liam entered the kitchen, he said, "Hey, you beautiful person," in his deep booming voice, giving me a big broad smile. He bent down for a kiss. "You are the queen bee. I brought you some chocolate mint ice cream." He knew that was my favorite flavor and that Peter was probably restricting me from such things.

I continued to devour the potluck spread of delicacies; Baby Em gave me an insatiable appetite! Since it was warm enough to gather outside, we carried our plates to the backyard. Just outside the door was a freshly tended garden plot with easy access to the kitchen, especially important at harvest time. Plant starts were peeking through the windows of a small greenhouse set off to one side of the yard. Beyond this area, we sat in a circle on logs surrounding the fire pit. Daffodils were growing around the edge of the property in front of a hedge of boxwoods, which provided privacy.

Blessings to Em

While standing in a circle holding hands and listening to the silence, Liam opened with a blessing from the tradition of his tribe. "This circle represents the earth, the four seasons, the stages of life, and the races of people."

He walked to the center of the circle and with great reverence gently continued, "Turn to face the East." He led us through facing each of the four directions, then the center, pausing at each one and praying.

"We give thanks to the rising sun, bringing us warmth and light. This is the place of new beginnings, and today we honor and send prayers for Em as he begins his earth journey." He looked warmly into my eyes, then at my belly, then caught the eyes of each person in the circle before looking skyward. I lifted my plate of food to toast the gods.

Liam continued, "Now turn to face South. Here is where the sun is at its highest point: the direction from which warm winds blow. We give thanks for the gift of life. From here we pray for world peace."

We were then directed to face west. "In this direction, the sun sets and darkness comes. This is the place of dreams, introspection, and the unknown. Here, we give thanks for the water of life and pray for purity, strength, and self-understanding."

Facing north, Liam spoke again: "North holds the spirit of the wind. Standing here we reflect on what we began in the east, in the morning of our youth. We give thanks for the great white cleansing wind. We pray for wisdom."

While we faced the center of the circle where Liam stood, he ended the prayers speaking both in English and his native Lakota language: "We honor all forms of life: other peoples, animals, birds, insects, trees and plants, rocks, rivers, mountains and valleys. We are interconnected. Thank you, Mother Earth and Father Sky. Great Spirit guide our hearts with love. To all our relations, Aho Mitakuye Oyasin."

After the beautiful opening blessing, we returned to the kitchen to gorge on the spread of healthy food: veggies, salad, wild rice casserole, sweet potatoes, nuts, and brownies. Liam said in his loud voice: "Peter, close your ears and close your eyes." He looked at Peter until he put his index fingers up to his ears, pushing them closed, and shut his eyes. Then Liam looked at me and whispered, "Samantha, let's not forget the mint chocolate ice cream."

Belly Cast

Everyone was smiling, laughing, and carrying on in delight. There was a glow around our connection. When we were full, we circled around in the living room holding hands, surrounded by house plants, vibrant with life. I lay in the middle of the circle on soft cushioning, my belly protruding skyward, the edges of blankets folded in towards me to create a makeshift nest. It was so sweet to be surrounded by this fun-loving, inspirational group, being spoon-fed ice cream, while Peter massaged my feet and toes. I was deeply moved by so much love in the air.

Angela used a layer of Vaseline to cover my belly: a balloon shaped protrusion that looked like it was going to pop. One by one, my friends picked up strips of gauze coated with plaster, dipped them in a bowl of warm water, and covered my belly with them. On the final layer they cut words out of the newspaper, dipping the strips in the wet, goopy plaster water, covering the curved belly bowl with a decoupage finish and shouting the printed words one after the other: "Coming Soon," while laughter was building, "Gas Goes Up," then "Encore," and "Hey everyone, look at this: Gold Star Meat." "Thanks be to God." "Closest to the Heart." "Breakthrough." Giddiness filled the air. "Still Showing." "Excavations." "Quick Consent." "Sacred." "Imagine." I was laughing so hard, I thought I might start labor, and I did dribble in my pants. "Zoning Change." "No. 1." "Functioning Fine." "Watch," and "Straight to the Source."

After the crescendo of the celebratory giddiness, when the plaster form with the decorated words had dried some, and in silence—all of us exhausted from laughing so hard—my friends carefully removed the sacred bowl from my abdomen. Then we all stood up and placed the bowl in the nest. Liam closed the circle ritual saying: "Blessings to the east, the south, the west, and the north. Thank you, Mother Earth and Father Sky. Please continue to protect us and bring greater peace to the world. Great spirit, we have opened our hearts and our hands as we welcome Em into this family of friends. We entrust into your hands the final delivery. Aho." We took a moment to breathe.

Get Some Sleep

We all agreed to meet the next day to help with the move to my new townhouse, then everyone slowly began to disperse. As I said my farewells, I looked at each member of my birthing team, entrusting them with my care through the pending birth process. We locked eyes, one by one, and shared heartfelt wishes.

"Ralph, thank you for helping me create life. We are so fortunate to have the opportunity to offer such a gift."

Ralph nodded and winked, while cocking his head to the side so his handlebar mustache stood in a 45-degree angle to the floor, and said, "Happy I got to be the sperm donor." I could see some warmth in his eyes, but that comment felt strange to me. Maybe it meant he was trying to distance himself from getting attached. By this point, "sperm donor" sounded like cold words—unlike "father" or "sacred giver."

"Peter, I'm counting on you, my dear," I said.

"Samantha, when have I ever disappointed you? Wait, let me rephrase that. You can count on me; you know that honey. And I will keep you well fed." I felt love flowing from his whole being as he stroked my hair and kissed me gently. "Goodnight," he whispered, hugging me goodbye.

Christine joined our hug and I said to her, "The show must go on," to which she replied, "Break a leg!"

Liam tooted his train whistle, giving me a wink, as he slipped out the door, disappearing into the night.

Vanna then held my hand, and Angela held the other, as the last exchange of words from this love fest were shared.

"Angela," I said, "I am honored and have no words to convey my gratitude for allowing me to be the carrier on this grand adventure with you." We teared up as she laid her hands on my belly, as if hugging Baby Em, then Vanna and I walked out hand in hand, sharing an unspoken connection, sisters forever. I savored this magical time, knowing things were about to change.

When Vanna dropped me off, she looked at me and started to cry. "Samantha, this is really touching me in the deepest way, and I can't stop wondering about my own birthmother. She abandoned me without keeping any contact. I want to try looking for her again. Will you help me?"

"Of course. I have a feeling we will find her. I love you. Good night."

"See you tomorrow. Love you. Nite."

In my role as an honorary auntie, I would know this baby born from my womb, something I thought would be emotionally helpful to him as he grew up. At the same time, I was feeling sad and concerned to hear Vanna talk about her feelings of abandonment. Now pushing 50, she still had a terrible longing to be connected to her biological parents. Would my child ever feel abandonment with what I thought was a protective and failsafe plan?

I was grateful for my friends, and all the roles they played, teaching me new perspectives on life as this journey evolved, while still mostly ignoring any warnings in this 11th hour, including from some of my well-meaning ecovillage friends. Although this caused me some hesitation and I wanted to be open to their experience and wisdom, I felt pretty close to being ready to welcome this new life in the way I had designed my plan.

It was time for some shut eye. I took off my loose, comfortable dress—one of my finds from the second-hand store—and warmed myself up under a thermal cotton sheet and the colorful blue and purple baby blanket my sister Jane had knit for Em. Starlight twinkled through the window frame. First, I rested my hands on top of my belly and felt the baby as he twisted, turned, and somersaulted. I had never been this close to anyone in my life, and never would be again. In the dark, I breathed for both of us, wrapping my arms around my belly to hug him as tightly as I could while rocking us both to sleep.

"Good night. Sweet dreams, Baby Em," I said softly.

2
Giving Birth to an Empty Nest

THE FOLLOWING DAY, WITH ONLY a few weeks to go until my due date, there still seemed ample time to get moved and settled into my townhouse. I was looking forward to finding a rhythm as "auntie" to this newborn soul and enjoy a closer proximity to Peter. Part of the purchase attraction was hearing passing trains nearby, a soothing sound that meant "home."

After a full day of moving boxes and furniture with the help of my birth team, I crashed at around ten o'clock. Within half an hour, I awoke to a strange feeling, like a punch in the gut. Twenty minutes later another cramping sensation had me doubled over in bed. "Should I call my midwife?" I wondered. For the moment I passed these off as Braxton Hicks contractions, not full-on labor pains. As the night wore on, with more interruptions, I wrote down the time of each gut-punch, trying to sleep between them. Had I brought on labor prematurely with the strain of the move? By 6 a.m., the painful contractions were ten minutes apart, so I called Peter to come be with me.

"Good morning, Peter Pan. Ready to fly? I've been having heavy contractions. Can you come over, like NOW?!"

"Good morning! Okay! Um, yes, I'll get dressed and be there soon. Holy moly! Bye, honey."

I called my midwife. "Sage, I've been having contractions all night, and waited to call you because it was so late last night, and I thought it was just false labor. I'm not due for two weeks, but the contractions are ten minutes apart."

"Samantha dear, you know you can call me anytime," Sage said. "It sounds like today's the day. Let me rearrange some things. Take a warm bath. It might alleviate the pain. Breathe. Hang in there. Call me back when the contractions are five minutes apart."

I fumbled with the phone and made quick calls to my birth team: Angela, Ralph, and my other friends. I told each of them I was in labor, and to wait for a call when the time got closer. One by one, we all went on red alert, dropping everything to rearrange our day. I wanted to call my mother, but I couldn't bring myself to listen to the heartbreak she was anticipating.

When Peter arrived, I was standing at my closet, naked, trying to figure out what to wear. I needed more time to get settled in my new home and to prepare, but here we were.

"Hi honey," I said with a weak smile. "Will you pick out something for me to wear? I can't think straight!"

We hugged, then Peter took a flowery Hawaiian muumuu off the hanger and went to fill the tub. The warm bath didn't help. I spent the morning and early afternoon moaning through each contraction. At 3 p.m. I called Sage. Halfway into my sentence a contraction hit and then I screamed. Peter took the phone and followed her instructions: "Bring her in now." He called Angela, who called Ralph, and the message was passed on through the phone tree. Everyone knew to meet at the hospital birthing center.

Off to the Hospital

En route to the hospital, off in the distance, I heard the familiar train whistle. Ah, that soothing sound. It flooded me with adventuresome travel memories. Then Peter said, "Oh baby, we gotta beat that train!"

"Take it easy," I said. "It'll be okay."

The daffodils on the roadside were nodding their pretty yellow bonnets, saying, "Yes, today is the day." As it happened, we were stopped for about 20 minutes at the train tracks. I could scream out when a contraction came, and no one would hear me. Then I could take a breath and use humming to distract myself. I fell into an altered state while continuing to reminisce about my fun early train hopping days, which helped me avoid thinking about the reality I was facing. Then "Ow, ow, ow, hurry!"

By the time we arrived at the hospital, reality had hit hard. "Please, baby, wait. You are too early and I'm not ready to let you go." I said to myself.

When I tried to walk into the hospital, it felt like my baby would just spill out. I was soon being wheeled to the birthing room. The baby's head had dropped further into my birth canal. The desire to stop the clock reminded me of when I went sky diving. Once I jumped out of the plane, there was no going back. It was free fall now as well.

Ready Or Not, Here He Comes!

My internal monologue went on, with delirium setting in between the screams. "Will someone get me out of here? I need time! What effing mess have I gotten myself into?"

Baby Em was making his appearance with a grand entry that would rock my world. I had talked to him and sung to him the whole time he was growing in my womb. I had explained that he would have a different mama who would raise him and love him as if he were her very own, silently reassuring him that I would always love him and that in my heart we would never be apart. But the hit I was getting now was that we were bonded, deny it or not. How would I ever separate myself from this new life that I had felt grow inside of me? All I could think was, "Let me off of this train!"

Another warm bath with various positioning gyrations to attempt getting comfortable seemed futile. Meanwhile my birth team had arrived. I hobbled back to the birthing bed. Soft classical music from "Miracles" was playing while Christine gently applied lavender essential oil under my nose. I tried breathing in the way I had been taught during childbirth classes, except when the sharp pains would hit, then I would forget and instead hold my breath. I tried squatting to let gravity help me, which only seemed to cause a strong pain in my back. It became unbearable.

"Please, give me an epidural." I shrieked.

"Samantha dear, you're doing great," Sage, said softly. "Look at me and breathe. He's almost here. It is too late for an epidural."

"OK, damn it! Give me something, anything, to knock me out!"

I had written a birth plan to include natural childbirth. Sage and another midwife teaming with her were at my side, both giving me reassurance. Even so, who can imagine this kind of excruciating pain ahead of time? I was beside myself, hearing the echo of what my friend told me: "Birthing will feel like peeling your eyelids backwards over the top of your head and down your body."

Only time would get me out of this unstoppable crisis. Angela and Ralph were attempting to be a good cheerleading squad. Peter was at my side massaging my head and encouraging me to scream out the pain like animals do, but I was so tired after 16 hours of labor; all that came out now were weak moans and whimpers.

When contractions hit, my feet pushed against the stirrups on the bed. Christine fed me teaspoons of mint chocolate ice cream, trying to be playful as she dabbed some on my nose. Liam brought his train whistle and played it softly like a flute, knowing it might soothe me. His big brown teddy bear eyes spoke of affection; they were full of desire to take the pain away. Vanna was sitting in a chair on the side of the room crying, holding her sock monkey, George, like a blankie. She knew nothing about her biological mother and was emotionally triggered by being there while I was giving birth. I clenched my teeth, bit my nails, and pulled on my hair.

Sage said, "Push. He's almost here."

"I can't anymore." I shouted.

"You can do it. Push."

Liam said, "I see his head with black hair." He started laughing.

My face was beet red from pushing. With the little stamina I had left, I gave a final push and out popped baby Em, with a head full of wet black hair.

Welcome to the World

Ralph hid his tears behind the movie camera while capturing his son's entry, jubilant to see his own DNA hatch before his eyes. Em was gently lifted and placed on my bare chest. I felt myself falling helplessly deeper in love. Angela cut his cord. There was so much jubilation in the room, but my thoughts were jumping to what lay ahead. My heart was breaking. I was exhausted, confused, and numb. My baby—someone else's baby now—would be going home in a few days with his adoptive mom.

Em was passed around in a circle of his new group of fans while I lay in bed trying to rest through the delivery of the placenta. They were all in awe as he looked at them, meeting the eyes of each person who held him. Then the nursing staff took some time administering his first health check. Finally, he was placed back on my chest, skin to skin. I held back the tears. I hadn't known that I could feel this deep of a love and connection to anyone. When I had agreed to have a child for my friend Angela, I hadn't seen this coming. It hit me hard.

Despite budding reservations about what I had agreed to do, I continued to go along with the plan to relinquish Em to his new mother after I was dismissed from the hospital. I had agreed to continue to give Em breast milk, either stopping by his new home to breastfeed or pumping and delivering it. I was prepared to be at Angela's beck and call for a few months, at the very least. How on earth would I do this?

These tender moments with my newborn, the feeling of Em's heart beating against my breast, the sweet newborn baby smell, the softness of his skin, his baby eyes looking at me, was an experience I knew I would never forget, imprinted into my whole being.

Before my birth support team left the hospital, I sang to Angela the song I had sung to her on her birthday:

"From you I receive…to you I give…together we share…and from this we live…"

"He belongs to the universe," Ralph said.

All Alone with My Grief

The team of us all being together in such intimate space came to an end. There were warm hugs goodbye, and everyone left so the baby and I could get a good nights' rest. I felt so alone. I clung to Baby Em as he slept in my arms. My body, now all mine, felt so very empty. My heart ached as the reality of the looming parting drew near.

I was worn out but needed to call my mother. "Hi, Mom. I only have a minute. I want you to know Em is a healthy and beautiful blue-eyed baby boy."

Her voice was choked, and in the same breath she chose to be supportive. "Samantha, I'm happy for you all and wonder how you are. I'm also curious about how things are being arranged with Em's new mother. Is she taking Em home soon?"

"Don't worry, Mom. He'll go home with her when I get released from the hospital. I'm okay. My heart is a little bruised and my tailbone too, so I get to stay here with Em and rest for a few days." I didn't dare share how I was really feeling. It was all matter of fact, just following the plan. I clung to the phone before hanging up. "Mom, I understand now. Thank you. I'm sorry, and I love you."

When it came time to register Em's birth, I gave him a sing-song name combining his biological father's name, Peter's nickname, and my last name. This name would be on his original birth certificate, one that I could have for my own records: Em Lynn Pan Song. With the adoption, his name would change soon. His original birth certificate would basically be null and void. "What's a piece of paper if you're not taking him home?" I sadly thought.

3
Kidnapped

ON THAT FIRST OVERNIGHT at the hospital when a nurse came in offering to take Em to the nursery, I groggily declined. She hugged me and whispered, "I was adopted. I think I understand, just in a different way."

I squeezed her hand and looked into her tearing eyes. "Thank you," I said, as I too began to cry. We sat in silence while we wept together. Her body shook as she tried to contain her sadness. We were overcome with grief, caught in a moment of deep-felt connection. Then she excused herself so she could regain her composure at work, quietly leaving the room.

Hospital Ward with My Newborn

The next morning, when carrying Em in the corridor, I was asked to lay him in a pushcart, for safety reasons. Did they think I was going to drop him? From then on, every time I ventured out of our room I had to first check to see if the coast was clear. Any time I was reminded about safety, I hmphed under my breath and returned to our room.

In that sacred container of the first few days, I hardly let Em out of my arms. At night I slept on and off while cradling him next to me, following his rhythm. I would gaze at him, feeling and watching his breath move. His belly button stump too would move, up and down. That remnant of our physical attachment was slowly dissolving. He was a champion breast feeder, instinctively knowing where to get the colostrum milk he needed to develop good immunity. While I was breastfeeding him, our eyes would lock. In those moments, I would die a little.

Nurses repeatedly offered to have Em taken to the nursery for newborns, insisting I needed to sleep. But why would I want to put him in that impersonal confinement area when he had just left a cozy womb? I heard other newborns crying out and didn't want to subject my son to what I thought was induced fear and overwhelm. Those babies were helpless. They needed their mamas to soothe them. Besides, I savored every second I had with him.

Visitors

A few of my birth team friends showed up, purposely spacing out their visits. First, Liam stopped by, tooting his train whistle softly. Then he sang us a tribal morning song. "We n' de ya ho, We n' de ya ho…" to greet the sun. He took Em into his arms touching his soft small lips while he continued to sing, "Ho ho ho, He ya ho… Ya ya ya…" He held Em and talked to him while I napped on and off. Later Angela and her parents arrived with daffodils. They were all ecstatic to see Em, of course. I was happy for them, but silently hurting for myself and my newborn.

In the afternoon, Vanna came by with George, her inseparable childhood stuffed monkey. She thought he should go home with Em, to be his protector. When alone with me, she kept tearing up. She had been searching for her biological parents on and off for what seemed like forever, first in secret so that her adoptive family wouldn't know—she didn't want to hurt them. After they both died, she became more public about her search. As Vanna was getting ready to leave, she held on to me and we cried together. I insisted that her beloved George go home with her. Peter walked in and brightened the sad mood, carrying two stuffed giraffes, a mama and a baby-one for me and one for Em. He said giraffes have the biggest hearts and reminded me about what a big heart I had in bringing the ultimate joy to the adoptive family. He tried to be playful, pretending we were in a zoo with a monkey and giraffes. Now, all we needed was a gorilla. Peter could not soothe my anguish.

There was so much love and, at the same time, so much grief. No other friends visited or called; why would they? This little boy with big blue eyes was not *my* baby. There were no more flowers and no more gifts to congratulate me. They all went to Angela's home.

I got used to being scolded for walking the halls while carrying Em. "Go to hell," was on the tip of my tongue, but I stayed quiet. My face said it all. I dreaded thoughts of going home without him. I wondered, "Didn't anyone understand? What did they know about me? Were they looking at me with disgust? Were they projecting, or was it me judging myself?

Angela came to the hospital the following morning for the discharge. I didn't show my deep distress. While holding Em, she asked me if I were available to take care of him on the weekdays until her replacement at school had been fully trained. I was honored that she asked me first, so, when we left the hospital, I was beside myself to be going home with Em. I hadn't scheduled anything else in anticipation of the now disrupted due date.

Buying Time from the Inevitable

I delighted in the extra time with Em. I could set my grief aside in the same basket of denial I had carried throughout my pregnancy.

We went for long walks, with Em absorbed in the newness of his surroundings, or asleep in the sling I carried him in. The skies seemed perpetually blue, and daffodils were still in bloom. On one of our outings, I picked us a bouquet of those yellow flowery bonnets, some to give to Em's father the next day (his favorite flowers), and some for the proud new mama.

On our outing the following day I dropped off those flowers where Lynn's father worked. Of course, he wanted to show off his progeny. Then we visited Vanna's clay studio where Liam was glazing a large vase. We put Em's footprints in the glaze, then imprinted them on the vase. While there, I glazed a clay trivet for Angela with Em's footprints. We matched the trivet to a cute little clay mug that Vanna had made with Em's new name, "Lynn," embedded into it.

On our daily walks we often went to sit by the train tracks and watch the trains go by, which was music to my ears, but too loud for Em. I had to put my fingers in his ears. Someday, he would get to hear stories about me and my train-hopping adventures.

Even though I lived near Angela, it worked better for me to stay overnight at her house. Em's sleep schedule was erratic, as expected. My freelance work schedule was flexible enough to put in hours as I was available.

There had been lots of support, trust, and love among the birth team all along the way. It seemed like that would continue. I felt honored to be playing this extended family role, knowing things would change, but not seeing an end to the beautiful connections.

We took baby pictures and sent out birth announcements with Em's new name. Angela had come up with the name Lynn, in honor of his biological dad, using part of his last name (Lynnwood). Lynn, of Celtic/Gaelic origin meaning "from the lake," was also a fitting name for a Pisces (the astrological sign depicted by a fish symbol). "Lynn" could now also symbolize the lake of tears I was shedding. This was so strange to me, since I had never been a crier.

Lynn was a peaceful baby, so quiet in his demeanor. He seemed so comfortable. I loved holding and snuggling him. When he would wake up at night, wide-eyed lying next to me, he didn't utter a peep; he mostly just stared out into his new world, then stared at me. His shining blue almond-shaped eyes seemed to glow in the dark and carried that same special glow in the daylight. I treasured every moment, treating each one as if it would be our last.

Sticking with "Best Laid Plans"

Before Em's birth, Angela, Ralph, and I had written a supplement to the adoption agreement, ready to submit to the Registry of Deeds office. Angela had been gathering the other legal adoption papers from her lawyer. Em surprised us with his early entrance. Little did we know that he, the universe, and God may have been orchestrating something from the heavens that would throw our best-laid plans into the ditch.

After the first few weeks of caretaking, the plan was that I would continue to provide pumped breast milk for Lynn, just as my childhood best friend June had done for three months after her son was born. She herself had been adopted from Korea. Then she repeated the cycle by giving up her own baby. Earlier in our conversations, before the birth, June told me that if she could handle it, I could too.

June was Deaf,[3] so I had to use a special video phone to call her.

---

[3] Carol Padden and Tom Humphries, in *Deaf in America: Voices from a Culture* (1988): "We use the lowercase "d" in the word "deaf" when referring to the audiological condition of not hearing, and the uppercase "D" in "Deaf" when referring to a particular group of deaf people who share a language: American Sign Language (ASL) and a culture. We distinguish them from, for example, those who find themselves losing their hearing because of illness, trauma or age; although these people share the condition of not hearing, they do not have the access to the knowledge, beliefs, and practices that make up the culture of Deaf people."

When I reached her one afternoon while Lynn was napping, I told her, "I am struggling and don't know what to do."

"Samantha, I understand. I have to confess that I have lived with grief every day since I relinquished my child all these seven years. On top of that is the grief of not knowing my own birth parents. I just thought you were much stronger than me and that you could handle anything."

"June, I can't handle this. It feels like an emotional time bomb went off inside me, and it won't stop. It is so hard," I whimpered.

"I know how hard it is. I breastfed my son for three months. If I could do it all over again, I wouldn't go through with the adoption. At least *you* still have time to change your mind."

"What?! I still have time to change my mind? I'm a little upset that you didn't tell me the truth before the birth. There's no guidebook for me to follow on this one and you're one of the people I depended on. It seems so surreal."

"Samantha, you were so convincing. I thought you could get through this more easily than I have. I'm sorry. Please forgive me. Thank you for being honest with me now. I love you.

"Love you, too, June. I'll let you know how things go."

"I am sorry, please forgive me, I thank you and I love you."[4] I had grown up using those four phrases, first with family, something my dad learned in WW II when he was in Hawaii, then used with friends. There were so many situations in life that needed those comforting words.

June's layered story had new meaning to me as I faced the grief of relinquishing my child. It was hard hanging up. I needed support

---

[4] See *completewellbeing.com* for more about *Ho'oponopono and the four phases that heal and help.*

big time. I had previously agreed that during the times I would be home from Belize, where I planned to return to volunteer for the winter, I could visit Lynn once a week. And once a year, when he was older, I could take him to meet his biological extended family in Maine.

After two weeks of caring for Lynn, with denial and shock wearing off in the midst of our looming separation, I could not bear to continue seeing him if I was going to follow the adoption plan. There was no Plan B. I had agreed that as soon as the legal papers were ready, I would sign them, but I couldn't wait any longer to fully cut the cord. My word was good, and I had no intentions of breaking a promise. So, I told Angela she had to take Lynn full time. I needed to get away to have space to heal.

Severing the Bond

I hoped I was doing the right thing for Lynn. I had read that, in some cultures, newborn babies stay in a quiet room for several weeks, usually alone with their mothers, as they adjust to life beyond the womb. My time with Lynn had been a sweet time with much closeness, but there had been lots of interruptions. I wondered how he would do with this transition.

Naivete had gotten the best of us. With deep hidden grief and fighting back tears, I hugged Lynn close to my heart, then handed him off to his new mom. Angela took charge, along with her parents, to give me as much time as I needed to recover.

Em was two weeks old on that spring equinox, which ironically happened to be the anniversary of Peter's father's suicide. This year we were sharing a "death" experience of a loved one together. I remember early in the pregnancy when I told him my due date. He had shuddered and said: "Do you remember what I told you that happened on that date?"

I said, "Your father."

He said, "Maybe my father is coming back to haunt me for not taking some responsibility; maybe he's wanting us just to have a baby the normal way."

"Please don't say that, Peter Pan. He sent a gift."

Apparently, Em chose not to claim that date to enter this life. Nothing like an early surprise, but now traumatic for me.

Letting go of my son felt like the death of Em—not our baby, but mine, a child born of my body after nine months within that dark harbor. I had been wrong to think that having a child simply meant an act of biology, and my heart shattered to consider that this baby would not grow up with me as his mother, in my home. No matter what, the bond between us was physically breakable, but underneath unbreakable. I was so utterly unprepared for this arrangement.

Separation Trauma

I asked myself, "Why aren't you bouncing back from this strange feeling of grief? What might Lynn be going through?" When I awoke each morning, I had dry heaves. I could barely get out of bed to go to the bathroom. My lifeline was the phone. While lying in bed I called everyone I knew for advice, and after that round I would call them again. I remember a $500+ phone bill. I felt unsettled in my new house, not yet unpacked from the move and too weak to deal with all the boxes. When Peter came over with a bouquet of daffodils, I threw them in the trash. He continued trying to comfort me, but I couldn't take it in. I was a mess. I fought my true feelings: I wanted my baby back! The situation created an immense strain on our relationship.

Vanna delivered dinners, with her fingernails full of clay after a day in the studio, bringing me the nourishment of food and friendship. In me she saw her own birthmother, who must have struggled to separate, and she realized that maybe her birthmom had loved her after all. She had long-held feelings of anger towards this unknown woman for abandoning her, and she lived with a deep inconsolable longing.

Vanna brought along George, her ever-faithful companion. He had been given to her by her birthmother when Vanna had been handed off to the adoptive parents—a hand-sewn friend that had been the birthmother's when she was a little girl. She still clung to this stuffed animal for comfort.

Peter and Christine's good friend, Harry, checked in on me daily that first week of separation. This became ongoing. He had moved to the area with them and found work as a pastor at a local church. The round bald spot on the back of his gray-haired head looked like a halo. It was easy to imagine him as an angel; he was kind and spoke with a gentle tone. Seeing me so distraught, but remembering meeting me as a different, happy and successful person, he had hope that I would regain my health.

At first, I didn't understand why Harry took me under his wing so enthusiastically but then learned how his own mother had abandoned him. He was raised by his grandmother. To make matters worse, he had been going through a rough divorce, and in that process was estranged from one of his three daughters. My situation had stirred up something big inside him. The balm he brought was for his own soul also.

Harry was sometimes successful in getting me out on hikes to scenic mountain trails and/or waterfalls. When he arrived at my house on warm, beautiful days with blue skies beckoning, he would have food and gear packed and ready for a day-long outing, escorted by his dog Cleo, who would lick me all over and join in wooing me out. But I was a walking zombie on those outings, feeling caught in a deep black death. Every day seemed like an eternity full of longing for my baby.

Harry had great patience and compassion for my sadness. Vanna, Peter, Harry, June, Liam—in one way or another, all of them had felt abandoned by a parent, and that had scarred them. How could I abandon Em? I started to question what I thought I knew about life. Where had my easy positive outlook gone? What kind of world were we living in that didn't prepare us for parenthood in all the unique ways it plays out? Maybe it's not possible. What I did know is there was no going back. I was a mother.

Lingering Discomfort

The dark discomfort lingered. I did a little bit of freelance interpreting work, but mostly found myself too weak to handle it. While waiting at medical checkups to seek help for my postpartum depression, sitting without my baby, with other women holding theirs, I would share my story openly. Some would fess up to postpartum feelings; mostly though, they made it look like things turned out hunky-dory, and after listening to me, they knew they were much better off.

I had a double whammy. Not only were my hormones out of whack, I was continuing to deal with my grief from the trauma of separation, with raging maternal instinct at play, all working against a creative plan that backfired. I wanted some kind of escape from this hell. Morning hangovers from this mixed psychological cocktail were accompanied by phantom pains deeper than a lost limb.

Whatever it was, the intensity was killing me. No amount of soul searching reached my despair.

I lived far away from family and my network of distant friends. Even with local friends, most felt helpless in the face of my unbearable distress. Either way, some were still full of I-told-you-so's (even if they hadn't vocalized it) about the choice I had made to have this baby and then relinquish my parental rights. In my desperation, only a week into my separation from Lynn, which already felt like an eternity, I called Angela. I wanted to sound strong, but I also wanted her to know the truth about what I was going through. My voice shook as I said, "Angela, this is Samantha. You know, I'm having a hard time."

"I'm sorry it's so hard, Samantha. Take your time getting through this. We are managing okay. My parents and friends are a big help."

"The reason I called, um, well..." I paused and took a deep breath.

"Samantha, what is it?"

"I was wondering if we could change the game plan and share custody of Lynn?" I blurted out.

"What?! Samantha, you know that wouldn't work. Remember what we agreed on? You said you were told this would be like a death. I know how strong you are. Why don't you take a vacation after we get the papers signed?"

"Angela, I'm just trying to find a way to fix my broken heart. This is harder than I thought it would be, but I guess I'll be okay." With every ounce of determination and conviction I could muster I caved in and said, "I'm sorry I'm so out of sorts. I just need a little more time to get over this."

I started scribbling on the yellow pad on my kitchen counter as I talked. I drew a butterfly and then around it a chrysalis. Then I drew a gorilla with the name Godzilla. I scribbled daffodils, daisies, and clouds, then added lightning.

Signing Adoption Papers

"I know you'll be okay. Can you come with me on Friday to my lawyer's office to sign the papers? Let's get that over with so you can move on."

"Um, yeah, sure. Will you pick me up? Please leave Lynn at home. I can't bear to see him for now, okay?"

When I hung up the phone, I ripped the drawings I made into shreds and cried. These days I cried alone a lot and then tried to put on a good face when others were around.

On April Fool's Day, with Lynn three weeks old, I pretended to be recovering nicely and consented to the adoption arrangements, signing away the rights to my baby. I knew from reading about adoption in my state that I had three weeks after signing papers to revoke this, but I thought with this major hurdle behind us, I would be able to move on, even if I had to force myself. April fools!?

Easier Said Than Done

Liam had been stopping by sporadically, and I trusted him with my true feelings. He patiently listened to my broken record while working at keeping his own PTSD about the separation from his mother at bay. It was triggering him to see me suffer so he enlisted Pastor Harry to give him support.

When I learned that Liam was consulting Harry to get some advice, I had all of us meet together to try to find a solution for my conflicted heart. I asked them to keep our conversations confidential. My question to Harry was, with two women wanting to lay claim on Lynn, me already having signed away my rights, what wisdom could he grace us with?

Harry shared "The Judgement of Solomon" story from the Bible about two women both claiming to be the mother of a baby. King Solomon suggested the baby be cut in half, giving each mother one half of the child. In the story, the birth mother stopped this from happening by giving the rival mother the child. From this loving selfless act, the birth mother proved herself the true mother, and King Solomon granted her the baby. This story wasn't my situation, of course, but I desperately wished and hoped that Angela would walk up to my door and gently offer Lynn back. Harry encouraged me to just go get Lynn, since Angela had not accepted the alternative I had offered. I still had a legal right to him.

I convinced myself that Harry's own projections and his unresolved desires to have a close connection with his absentee mother had perhaps gotten mixed in with his advice. *Perhaps*, I wondered, as the cracks of light tried to pierce into the darkness shrouding my heart.

Angela stayed away from my struggle, focusing on caring for her newborn son. She didn't have time to hear the murmurs of my misery being exchanged throughout the pipeline of mutual connections. How could she feel like the authentic mom and acknowledge my longing at the same time? Something was amiss.

The story continued to unfold. My boyfriend Peter, who had been willing to be supportive in this whole process, was now feeling weighed down by the heaviness of my lingering distress. Our relationship was crumbling, and I didn't know how I could weather another loss.

Ralph, the donor dad, tried to be supportive. He stopped by on a few occasions to visit Lynn at Angela's, and while in the neighborhood came to check on me. I didn't know him well. As far as I could tell, Ralph was smart, cared about the environment, had good politics, and took care of his health. We shared important values but, if you recall, I wasn't attracted to him on an emotional level. Our relationship was more of a friendly business-like connection. He wasn't invested in me. Given all that, early on I had figured this whole arrangement would be a safe bet; he would be the father of a child I would gift to Angela, who would then raise this child with minimal responsibility from us. Angela had endorsed my selection. Easy peasy, *right?*

Turning the Tide

One afternoon, in desperation, I called Ralph at work, and asked him if he could come and talk to me in person. "I'm obsessed with grief about *our* son and am having a hard time getting over it. How are you feeling?"

"Me, too, Samantha," he replied. "I didn't expect to feel this way but I'm okay. I'm really busy at the moment. I can stop by this evening if you want."

"I'm so confused, conflicted, and my body is so weak. Maybe I need more time to recover? It hasn't even been a week. It's just strange, and yes, please stop by."

When Ralph showed up, he could see my bloodshot eyes as he approached my bedside, where I lay covered with crumpled blankets and wads of wet tissues strewn around. I didn't have the strength to get up, much less the wherewithal to know what to do with my changed life. I told him at times I would lie as if frozen in bed, with my heart saying, *Go get Lynn*, while my mind and body had their own blockades saying, *No breaking promises.* My hair tangled, my heart in tatters, I looked exactly as I felt. My lavender nightgown, soaked in sweat and tears, clung to me like a second skin.

"Samantha, I've given this some thought, and I can go get Lynn and bring him to my house. Then we can use the remaining time before things are final to figure out what we want to do."

"Really, Ralph, you could do that?" I cried. I threw my arms around him and gave him a deep hug from which he wiggled free. Adoption revocation was almost unheard of. At least I had never heard of anyone doing such a thing. "It would be so unfair to Angela and her family, and they wouldn't willingly give up Lynn," I thought. The clock was ticking. We had ten days to decide. Ralph's housemates had just had a baby a few weeks earlier and perhaps they would step in and assist. He had fallen in love with Lynn also. It was a bit surreal, and, in my stupor, I agreed to have Ralph do whatever he could. It didn't fully register that this was even possible.

Later Peter, who lived next door to Ralph, called me and asked, "What is going on, Samantha? Ralph just walked into his house with a crying baby, and it's not his roommates' new baby!"

The scene reminded me of a cartoon story of victims, heroes and villains. Dudley Do-Right from the Bullwinkle TV series rescues my baby! Ralph had Lynn at his house and was scrambling to set up his household to care for him, with the help of his housemates and some help from Peter. Theirs was a labor of love, yet it was called a kidnapping by the bewildered adoptive family.

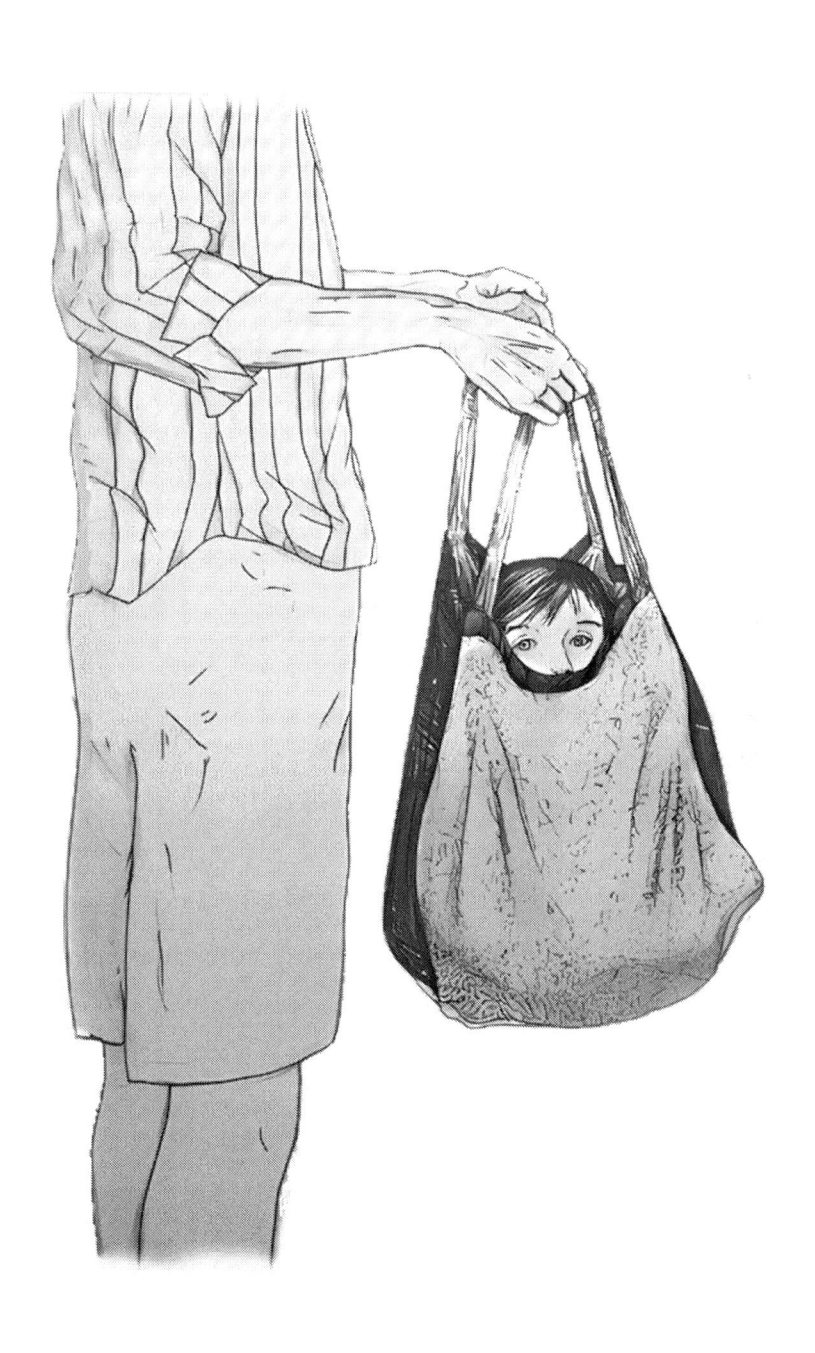

Lynn Song, artist

4
Hell's Roller Coaster

WHILE LYNN WAS ADJUSTING to living at Ralph's house, I laid around in bed at my place, recovering from what seemed like a bad train wreck. On the outside, I looked as normal as I ever had—a 33-year-old woman, strong and athletic. Every morning I muscled enough energy to at least tie my hair in a French braid, brush my teeth, put on a fresh cotton blouse and blue jeans. On the inside, holy terror was having a heyday.

For those first few days, it took all the strength I had to go visit Lynn. On my first visit when I walked in my heart sank as I saw Lynn off in the corner of the room sitting alone in an infant seat. He was being cared for by Ralph's housemate, also a new mom. Ralph was away for long hours focused on getting his research published. The new mama was doing her best being "supermom." While she was breastfeeding her son, Lynn had his bottle propped up with a towel, his head tilted sideways. As I picked him up, I felt so sad for him, and for all of us trying to manage his care. I rocked him until exhaustion overtook me, then handed him to his caregiver who now had her hands free and went back home to rest so I could face whatever was next.

I heard from Peter that Lynn was having bouts of projectile vomiting, which some saw as funny and entertaining, but I knew it was a stress reaction from all that this new soul had been through. It didn't seem right to me to have created so much unpredictability, especially for my baby.

Guilt and Maternal Instinct Duking It Out

Instead of feeling relieved to have Lynn in our care, I was worried about his future with a mom whose health wasn't bouncing back and a busy dad who was relying heavily on housemates. Besides, I couldn't stop ruminating about Lynn's adoptive mom and her family, who had been preparing for this baby for long months before his birth. How must *they* feel? Angela hadn't called me since Ralph had taken Lynn from her and was dealing with her own grief and loss. I continued to have a heavy case of guilt for breaking our agreement, and for how this was impacting Angela, and *all* involved. I kept it hush hush from my family. I didn't have the energy to hear any reactions, good or bad. It was a ginormous nightmare.

I went as far as asking Peter if he would be willing to be a stepdad and help me raise Lynn, suggesting it could enliven our relationship. He held his stance to remain free of raising children, and I could feel him distancing himself from me and this emotional roller coaster. We had been on the brink of breaking up before the birth, both moving in different directions, but I had needed him, and he had hung in there. Now, when I needed him more than ever, he was backing away to regain his own strength. He certainly was not available to take on the kind of responsibility I was asking for. Breaking up was another big loss.

"Goodbye, Peter. I'm sorry. Please forgive me. Thank you. I love you."

On the fourth day of having easy access to Lynn, when my despair had not budged, I slowly braided my hair and put on my running shoes. I dragged my deadweight body over for a visit, then put on my friendliest smile, but all the sunshine evaporated as soon as I opened the door.

I found Lynn lying awake, a pacifier in his mouth, quietly entertaining himself in his infant seat while Ralph was sitting at his desk nearby doing paperwork in his office. This new arrangement amid the whole situation was continuing to torture me, no matter how I tried to rearrange things to alleviate the pain.

In desperation I said to Ralph, "I've told you I can't seem to shake away the misery I feel in my whole body and soul; it haunts me. I know we are not ready to be parents. It will be better if we give Lynn back to Angela."

Ralph was reluctant. "Maybe my parents can come and help."

I raised my voice in opposition, "That is unrealistic! They aren't going to quit their jobs and relocate. And we can't be moving Lynn through so many different hands, creating such stress and strain on him and others who didn't sign up for this. His needs are not being met! I don't know how I can take care of him with how awful I feel. I don't even know what is wrong with me!" I whimpered.

Peter was next door, so I called him over to help me reason with Ralph. After some negotiating assistance from him, Ralph admitted we weren't ready to take on this responsibility and with my pleading, reluctantly gave in.

Please Take Him Back

When I called Angela on the phone, I begged her to listen, then promised her that I was truly committed to the adoption this time. To get a further vote of confidence I shared that I had called her lawyer, to let *her* know what I was doing, asking her to get the paperwork ready. I told Angela that my sister Joan, who lived in the next state over, offered to care for Lynn until the adoption was final, to help smooth the process and give her reassurance. Joan had promised to keep this all under wraps from my family.

We agreed to the new plan. Angela and I were feeling a little shell shocked and making big decisions on the fly. In these moments I felt connected to her again.

By the time Joan and her family drove over from several hours away, I was able to convince Angela to trust me, saying it would be better psychologically for Lynn to return directly to them, "…and please take good care of him." Joan and her family helped reunite Lynn with them. I was too heartbroken to face the separation.

"Goodbye Lynn. I'm sorry. Please forgive me. Thank you, and I love you." I would get a copy of all the adoption papers I had signed in a week. This would be a record I could keep or burn.

Teeter Totter

What had driven me to want to put the brakes on the adoption plan was the unexpected deep longing for my baby. I had tried to deny the awakened instinct that stalked me. I hadn't been able to resist the pull. When we got Lynn back, I felt intensely overwhelmed and guilt-ridden. Added to the confounding mixture of confusion for taking him away from my dear friend was the punishment I gave myself for breaking a promise. It had not brought me anticipated relief. I still felt like hell, both physically and emotionally, often hardly able to function.

Unable to quell the raging storm, it only made sense to me for us to return Lynn to Angela, who had a stable home and lots of support. I just needed to give myself more time to adjust and heal. "Things cannot get worse," I had thought.

Following my relinquishing him again, was a tsunami of heightened longing and self-loathing. What had I done so wrong to have to experience this living hell? Had I been having too much fun in my life and didn't deserve it? I vowed to stay away from Lynn until I felt better. All the king's horses and all the king's men could not put me back together again.

Over the next week, while the revocation clock was still ticking, I stayed away from visiting Lynn. Peter, who had been my steady and trusted boyfriend of the last year, was staying out of the picture. I wondered what wound this had opened for him. My birthing team had disbanded—only an adoption ad hoc committee, really—friends who hadn't signed up for more than that. But dammit! Why couldn't they weather the unpredictable outcome with me? Why did I have to suffer so much alone?

Other close friends were burning out on my ongoing sob story. I called everyone left in my phone book and laid the same rant on them. Despite the hodge podge of support I was getting, I was still extremely confused. The wall I had spent 9 months building to protect me from any attachment had been hit by a bomb and was now a pile of rubble. There I was standing naked with my raw emotions exposed. No one could take away the pain. Where does one begin to pick up the pieces?

There was only one person left to call: my childhood sweetheart, Dave, with whom I'd broken up over the issue of having kids. June would have his number. After wrestling with that possibility though, my heart already wrung out, I decided I couldn't bring myself to call him. I didn't need the love we had for each other adding to an already complex mix of emotional upheaval.

Most of my siblings were keeping quiet at the moment, watching this unfold from afar, certainly gossiping among themselves. My sister Marie, though, continued to send me cards with comforting quotes from *A Course in Miracles*.

The gangster fraternal twins of guilt and longing were camping on my doorstep, invading my house and taking over my mind. They wouldn't let me sleep! Not getting enough sleep is used to torture people. And postpartum depression mixed with relinquishment is its own form of PTSD. It is more common when surrendering babies than people will admit. For me, the intense feelings erupted over and again, with a growing vengeance against myself.

Birthmother Outcry

Driving home from running errands on a sunny spring day, I saw Angela carrying Lynn in a cloth sling—a proud new mama out for a stroll. She didn't see me. Only weeks earlier I had carried Lynn in the same baby sling. That was my baby she was carrying! It was surreal! When I got home, I went berserk. I grabbed the phone to call an adoption agency and asked to talk to a counselor. When the friendly woman's voice came on, I asked point blank without any introduction why they tell women who are getting ready to relinquish their children that it will be like a death.

I was told, "Because it is that painful, like a death."

To which I exploded: "To hell with that. There was no closure. My son did not die. It feels like having someone missing in action!" I yelled, then took a breath trying to calm myself, and while whimpering asked, "Have you ever heard of anyone revoking an adoption, and can you help me?"

"I'm sorry ma'am, we only work with women who are our clients and are ready to relinquish their babies."

Hanging up on her wasn't polite, but I had no more words, and I was too worked up to be civil. I knew she wasn't to blame. The bigger business of adoption was much more complex.

I had to somehow convince myself that revoking the adoption was no longer an option. I searched for other resources and found an adoption support group. Birthmothers were welcome. I would not be judged.

But damn! The meeting was a week away, which sounded like an eternity. It would be past my deadline to revoke the adoption, but I knew I needed their support and understanding to get past this.

Tick Tock Tick Tock

As the deadline for revoking the adoption closed in on me, I couldn't stop thinking about it. I was doing everything I could to stay away from Lynn, to let him settle in with his new mom. I could bounce off the walls in the privacy of my home without Angela knowing. But, while up against the time limit for revocation and in my weak state of health, I had my neighbor drive me to the courthouse to pick up adoption revocation papers, just in case I needed them.

The unfriendly secretary at the courthouse told me, "Nobody ever revokes an adoption. I don't even know if I can find paperwork for that. Young lady, do you know what you are doing?"

"I know exactly what I need madam sergeant and was told your office had the right form for me to fill out," I snapped back.

After shuffling through files, then walking to another file cabinet where I could see her shuffling some more, she found the form. She scowled while handing it to me. The way she treated me made me wonder if she had a personal connection to the adoption arena. I had two days until midnight on the final day to deliver the witnessed, signed, and notarized papers.

That night my hands were shaking as I held the revocation paperwork, reading it over and over again, as if memorizing it. I finally shut my eyes, lowered my head, and held the application papers over my heart. I fantasized about a kind way to get Lynn back, thinking,

"If I went through with this, how would I do it? What the hell would I say? Who would go with me? Why can't I just call Angela and talk with her like we used to talk? Why doesn't she get how hard this is?!"

The last possible day to revoke the adoption came. I had set up several late afternoon and evening appointments four hours away just to force myself to go through with my promise. I would be out of town at important meetings at Gallaudet University, in Washington, DC (the only Liberal Arts college in the world primarily for Deaf students). I had slowly been moving forward recruiting students to spend a semester in Belize, working with me on opening a school for deaf children there. I thought I could distract myself with meetings and interviews with prospective interns, inwardly reasoning that I had to be somewhere, so I couldn't break my promise to Angela. I would stay busy, running ahead of my emotions to keep from screaming, or weeping, or tearing out someone's eyeballs, most likely mine.

The Storm

I left town in the morning with a heavy heart. It was a warm 75 degrees and muggy. About 50 miles away, boogeymen showed up in the form of thick cone-shaped black thunderclouds looming in a yellow-orange sky. Tornado weather. I swear I saw the Wicked Witch of the West, along with Toto, bust through those black clouds, and I heard her cackle: "He's mine, he's *all* mine!" followed by her terrifying laughter. I felt as if daggers were being thrown at me from the sky. This imagined taunting poked a big hole in my defenses. What then erupted was a hidden rage I couldn't keep contained, and I became even more determined to go back and retrieve my son.

I stepped on the gas. My face was wet with tears. At the next exit I got off the highway and turned around to head back south. The skies were threatening imminent rain. I felt really scared. I imagined going to the police to ask them to escort me to Angela's house, arriving with papers in hand. It had to happen that day, some time before the clock struck midnight. How could I ever let myself do such a thing, though? But I was now on the highway driving south towards home and still had time to contemplate my options. In less than a half hour, I was heading off the highway to head north again. I don't recall the number of times I zig-zagged like this. I turned back and forth, with new surges of frenzy popping up presenting confounding and complex scenarios. I finally pulled over to try and gather my thoughts and make a good decision. I dozed off, emotionally spent, and too exhausted for anything to make sense.

When I woke up, I was confused to find myself parked on the side of the highway. Where was I? I knew I had gone mad. If there had been any highway patrol officer around to see this, I would have been hauled off to the loony bin. I couldn't go get Lynn, yet I had to. How could I be so conflicted?

There was still time for me to get to DC. As I made my last attempt to head north away from home, it started pouring. In my madness, with a constant stream of tears running down my face, blurring my vision, I pressed my lips shut to shield my mouth from the slime dripping from my nose as I floored the gas pedal.

Just up the road I started to speed past a semi-truck on the right side while he was inching his way into the right lane. Surely, he saw me?! Hard splashes of water hit my windshield as this metal beast continued to run me off the road. I moved over to the shoulder flooring the gas pedal, going faster to fully pass him and barely missing the front right side of his truck. Through the rearview mirror I could see his headlights flashing on and off high beam and what looked like gnashing teeth above the truck's front bumper. The driver honked long and hard, bringing me briefly back to my senses. I was not the only one on the road but had been driving like a maniac who owned the highway with no regard for others. That was a close call! Nothing like a fatal accident could have been the final determinant.

Defeated

Further down the road I stopped at a rest area to settle myself down and pee. Only a few cars were parked in the lot. I got back in the car, shut the door, and then in this state of shock, passed out. When I woke up it was dark. In my stupor, I engaged the engine so I could read the time. As I finally made it out, I realized that I had missed my meetings. Sitting there calculating my next move, I also realized it was too late for me to make it back home to deliver the revocation papers. I sat there and sobbed.

With my physical, mental, and emotional energy spent, I grabbed my sleeping bag from the back seat and laid it out on the passenger seat, adjusting the seat as flat as it would go. I crawled over the gearshift and brake lever into the mummy bag and spent the night tossing and turning, sleeping on and off, a whimpering mess.

In the morning I awoke to a police officer knocking on my window, checking to see if I was OK. "Thank you, officer, I'm just going through a rough patch. I'll be fine…" then muttered under my breath, "…when I'm dead." I threw up my hands in defeat. I hadn't made it to either destination. My time had run out. The window of opportunity to revoke the adoption was gone forever.

After that stormy night, I called to apologize to the university staff and students for standing them up, returned home, and got nursed by Vanna. Christine came over, too, reminding me that I was a mom, and telling me the feelings I had were normal. "Samantha, you are NOT crazy," she said, hoping I would believe it.

Denial

Even though the sand had run out on the revocation hourglass, the fantasizing about getting Lynn back continued.

Despite my closed window of opportunity, Christine offered to clear out a room in her home for Lynn and me, giving me support while I recovered. What were we thinking? Were we in denial?

A few days later Christine and I received a warm welcome at my first ever adoption support group. There were birthmothers, adult adoptees, and adoptive family members. How refreshing it was to finally be in a place where people understood me. When I asked the birthmothers how long it would take me to get over my loss, they looked at each other and then in unison said, "Never." They sent me home with two things that would make a difference in how things played out.

One of the gifts they gave me was the book, *The Primal Wound,* by Nancy Verrier. From the moment I opened it that night I could not put it down. In the morning I could hardly wait to call Vanna. "You've got to see this book I got at the support group last night. I haven't slept a wink. The book is mind blowing!"

To my amazement I was able to track down the author. I gave her name to directory assistance and said she lived somewhere in northern California. I dialed her number and was even more shocked to get a live answer. "Hello?"

Even though it was an early weekday morning on the west coast, Nancy was willing and available to spend time on the phone with me. She listened attentively as I blurted out my plight.

From a clinical standpoint, she was the first person to fully acknowledge and understand my erratic behavior and my deep pain. The kindness and understanding she shared was a balm for a deeply wounded spirit. I will never forget the fresh insight and understanding she offered, and the opening in my heart that her words found.

Nancy's expertise was in separation trauma, particularly as it related to adoption wounds. She had firsthand experience with these concerns as the mother of two daughters, the first of whom was adopted. This was the focus of her psychotherapy practice. We set up another phone appointment for later in the week.

Despite low energy and wanting to be done with the complexity of it all, and just when I thought the relinquishment of my son was settled for a second time, somewhere deep in my soul I was being led to another shore. My time was up; didn't I get it? I was fooling myself: one minute trying to convince myself I could move on, and the next entertaining and even seeking a way to reverse the adoption. Confusion and overwhelm were my constant companions. The unfolding drama had its way of changing course—a roller coaster ride that had me waking up literally vomiting.

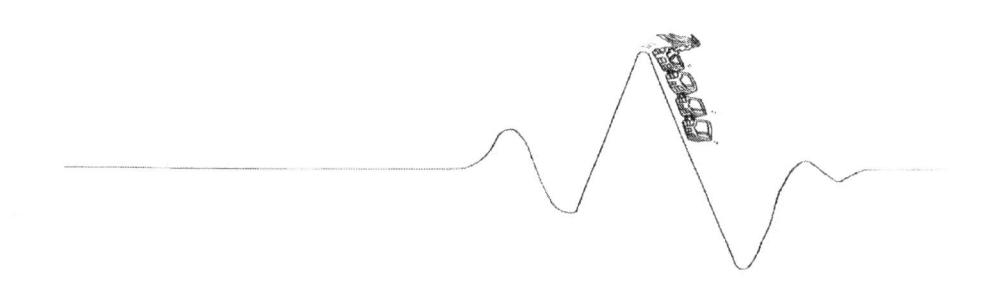

Lynn Song, artist

5
Adoptees, Birthmothers, and Adoptive Parents

BEFORE GOING TO BED I would often read something from my extensive collection of quotes and poems, a treasure trove that I had started in grade school. These words were guideposts and brought solace—my committed companion throughout the years that was there whenever I needed it, especially in my darkest hours. A poem resonating with me at that moment, in the depths of my despair, was another from Rumi:

Let yourself be silently drawn by the strange pull of what you really love.
It will not lead you astray.

What did I really love? More than anything, I had no doubt about the love I had for my baby. During my pregnancy, I had read many articles and books about open adoption that included flowery language about their merits—the bells and whistles talk. I read about selfless acts of love in relinquishment and the joy that comes in helping create a family. All along I had believed I could give birth, hand my baby off, and then return to my former life without a second glance. I was so naive. I had outright refused to read or listen to any opposing perspectives that did not fit my stance on the matter, so I found myself on a steep learning curve.

Valuable Insight

From Nancy's book and website,[5] I learned about the adoption "triad." There were perspectives on adoption from the standpoint of adoptees, adoptive parents, and biological/birth parents; some of the points had never occurred to me. Part of me wanted to keep the blinders I had on and put the story behind me. Try as I might, I could not wake up from the nightmare. I found myself facing a scary new reality. In my head I still wanted to be convinced that I had done the right thing from the get-go of this grandiose idea, so I could go back to my happy and free pre-pregnancy life. Was there a way I could continue merrily on my way and return to my work in Belize? Evidently not.

I learned that there is political correctness in adoption terminology. Had I given him up, relinquished, surrendered, or abandoned him? Was I wanting to take him back, or revoking the adoption? The battle of opinions between support for my altruistic gift, in contrast to the opposite perspective, made it seem that, no matter what I did, someone would always judge it as selfish and irresponsible. The crossfire now was between "Am I keeping him?" and "Am I giving him up?" There was no way I could win. It was truly a double bind. What would be best for my baby? If he grew up thinking I abandoned him, how would this affect his life?

In the Position Statement from Nancy Verrier's website, I read:
> *Every child who is separated from his or her biological mother will experience abandonment and loss.*

---

[5] Verrier, Nancy. Quotations are from an archived website. Parallel information is available in her book: *The Primal Wound: Understanding the Adopted Child* (Gateway Press, 1993). Used by permission from the author.

I learned:

> *Few dare give voice to that which they know in their hearts: that the connection between biological mother and child is primal, mystical, mysterious, and everlasting... So deep runs the connection between a child and its mother that the severing of that bond results in a profound wound for both, a wound from which neither fully recovers...*
>
> *This wound...is experienced not only as a loss of the mother, but as a loss of the Self, that core being of oneself which is the center of goodness and wholeness.*

It blew my mind to read:

> *There will be a difference between the environment of security and safety of being with the mother with whom an infant was prenatally bonded, and the anxiety and uncertainty of being with biological strangers (who may also leave at any time).*
>
> *It is important to recognize that the adoptee was present when the substitution of mothers took place... It wasn't a concept to be learned or a theory to be understood, it was a traumatizing experience about which the adoptee may have persistent and ambivalent feelings, all of which may be legitimate... Their feelings are an appropriate response to the most devastating experience one could ever have, the loss of the mother.*
>
> *The adoptee's loss must be acknowledged, validated, and worked through, so that they can gain a new attitude toward it and begin to gain a sense of Self (who they are), self-esteem (how they feel about themselves), and self-worth (how they believe they are valued by others).*

There was no escaping the facts.

Only when we set aside our denial…when triad members acknowledge their pain, and when clinicians recognize the differences between biological and adoptive families…can we proceed down the path to healing with understanding, insight, honesty, and courage.

I Need to See a Lawyer

So many questions were running through my mind. What was I supposed to do now? How could I help my son with the kind of unresolved trauma he would have to live with? Was the damage already done? I felt the trauma of the separation myself, which had not gone away, and as I read about the impact on adoptees, I just got sadder. Had I hurt Lynn in my ignorance? I needed to talk to Nancy again.

In the meantime, I made an appointment with a new lawyer, just in case. I wanted to know if there was any way to get Lynn back (plead temporary insanity?), or if I could formulate a proposal for Angela to reconsider joint custody. I remembered that on the day we had signed adoption papers, I was asked to leave the room while Angela and her lawyer stayed there. When I asked why I needed to leave, I was told that the next part of the meeting had nothing to do with me. Before I stepped out, I asked for copies of the papers I signed and was promised they would be mailed to me. At the time, though, it all felt strange to me; I was too exhausted to question them further. Something felt terribly wrong. What had I done? Could it be undone?

6
Four-Leaf Clovers

I CALLED MY EXTENSIVE quote collection my *Bible*. It brought me solace on a daily basis. Reading the quotations and poetry could temporarily distract me from my self-sabotage and negative thinking. I leaned on this treasury. *The Invitation* by Oriah Mountain Dreamer gave words to help me honor my calling. I read:

> *I want to know if you can disappoint another to be true to yourself; if you can bear the accusation of betrayal and not betray your own soul.*

Follow Up with Nancy

The next time I talked to Nancy, I asked her what she thought would be best for Lynn, given that the adoption process was well underway, and that I was very hesitant about trying to stop it again. Besides, I believed I no longer had legal grounds for such. My three-week time limit to revoke the adoption had run out. I wanted to give *her* the answer, even if I was wrong, before she said anything.

Nancy said it was always best for children to be with their birth families unless those families were incapable of taking care of them and couldn't give them a healthy home. She also reiterated what she wrote in her book: that since we had been separated, there had been a "primal tear" in our attachment and that someday my son might want to revisit this trauma in order to heal it. In the meantime, he would have an unconscious wound, a cellular memory of the separation. He might be angry at me, perhaps not being able to verbalize it, but might act it out. This unresolved separation trauma could play itself out over and over in Lynn's future relationships. Trust had been broken.

Nancy asked me if, given what I now knew, would I be following up with the appointment I had made with a lawyer? The conscious practical side of me was saying leave it alone, while the unconscious pull and struggle were always present. Her words pierced through me and echoed in my head.

I thought I wanted to hear that Lynn would be fine. I would get over this in time, and I could go back to Belize where I was gearing up to open the school for deaf kids. Ultimately, I wanted to hear that we would both be okay. I argued, saying that Lynn was bonded with his new family now and it was too late to go back. I tried to put words into Nancy's mouth.

She challenged me though, saying that bonding is what happens in utero and that Lynn had perhaps attached to the family, but no one could replicate a biological bond. Lynn knew my smell; he knew my heartbeat…

Dear God, now what? I felt anger welling up inside. I was full of blaming myself for not being strong enough to handle the life I had created. I wasn't having a polite conversation with myself. My mother used to use the word *shit* repeatedly when she got mad. I gave myself permission to say it, "Shit, shit, shit, SHIT!" I needed to let go and express myself. There was undoubtably a lot more ammunition from where that was coming from.

"Thank you, Nancy. I'm sorry Lynn, and please forgive me. Thank you. I love you, Lynn."

Seeing Lynn Again

Five more weeks had passed, and Lynn was now two months old. I thought I was ready to visit him and could be strong. As I was gearing up to see him, considering everything I was learning, I knew I would have to pretend to be better. Angela had given me permission to take Lynn for the afternoon, so Harry and I decided to take him downtown to an art festival.

My heart raced with anticipation and excitement in seeing Lynn then melted when he was placed into my arms. He had grown some, and his head was healing from the small, dry flaky scabs of cradle cap. His black hair was softer. He was the most beautiful baby in the world!

Lynn and I smiled and cooed at each other during the whole afternoon. I didn't want to put him down, so I paced myself with him in my arms, sitting some and resting along the way. I was fascinated watching him learn how to maneuver his hands. He'd squeal with surprise and excitement at all the new stimulation. Wide-eyed, yet calm, he took in the spectacle. I especially loved watching his facial expressions—a gaping mouth, a yawn, drools, pressing his lips together then turning them inside his mouth, pushing his tongue out—practicing all the moves a baby's face can make.

There were colorful booths donning various crafts on display and for sale. Street performers were spread out in the park, playing stringed instruments and drums, while jugglers performed. We danced and sang to the music. As we passed a man carrying a live monkey, I said, "Look, Lynn, it's a monkey." I guided his hand to softly pet this new furry friend. He squeezed the monkey's fingers, and the monkey shook Lynn's hand. They peered into each other's eyes and made funny sounds at each other.

As I ran into friends, I acted like a happy, proud and confident mom. It was a fun surprise to bump into my midwife, Sage. She had heard I had been having a tough time. When she realized it was Lynn I was holding, her eyes watered up and she held back tears. I wanted to inquire. I handed Lynn to Harry for a moment. Lynn reached back for me. I said in a high, mommy-toned reassuring voice, "I'll be right back Lynn honey."

Harry distracted Lynn, turning around and walking back to touch the monkey again while I stepped away.

"Sage, are you OK?"

"Hey Samantha, I've been thinking about you a lot and wanted to check up on you, but I was afraid to call. Hearing about your difficulty with your separation from Lynn set off some deep emotions buried inside me."

"Really? How does that relate to Lynn? I have a big decision to make soon."

"My mom got sick soon after I was born," Sage said. "I was separated from her and was passed around to various family members for a few months. I'm in counseling now, learning how that set the stage for an insecure attachment, having further implications in my life. I worry about Lynn and you. The adoption isn't final yet, right?"

"I'm still trying to figure things out, Sage, and I'm worried about us too. Can I meet you sometime for tea?"

"Call me soon. I'd like to say more, but I know you've gotta go," she said.

We made our way back to Lynn, walking with an arm around each other's shoulders. Sage shook Lynn's hand and smiled at him, then nodded at us. I briefly introduced her to Harry, then she waved and went on her way.

"Halo Harry," as I liked to call him—my tried-and-true friend—had continued to spend time with me throughout this ordeal, never tiring of my despair, just there with an open heart.

Helping someone else distracted him from the pain of his divorce process that he was in. I felt fortunate to have his support in the midst of his own sadness.

The afternoon ended too soon and I didn't want to take Lynn back to Angela. That day with my son ripped off the scab that had begun to form over my heart. I later heard from a friend that after I dropped Lynn off, he cried inconsolably. When I was alone that night, I did too. I knew Lynn remembered who I was, and I missed him so.

Where is My Copy of the Adoption Papers?

I couldn't stop wondering if there was a way to get Lynn back. Twice I had followed up with Angela's lawyer to find out why copies of the adoption papers had never been sent to me. On the first call she said she had been busy and it slipped her mind. On the second call she made another promise via her secretary to send them. I had less and less trust in her. Why would I believe her now? I suggested to the secretary that I come to the office directly, today, now, so that she could make copies of the papers I had signed. The lawyer then got on the phone and assured me that the papers would be sent in the mail the next day, so I waited, and several days later I finally received them.

I combed through the adoption papers. Then I read the copy I had of the adoption statute, another gift that had been given to me at the adoption support group, which I hadn't fully understood until now. It said that after the Home Study was delivered, the biological parents had an additional five days to revoke an adoption, beyond the three-week limit after signing adoption papers. I searched for but could not find the Home Study paperwork. My heart raced. I was so scared; my body was shaking. What if I could really get him back?!

A Home Study is part of the legal adoption process, and it concludes with a written report by a caseworker. This extensive report is an in-depth study on the adopting family that includes a family background check, financial statements, education and employment records, relationships and social life, daily life routines, parenting experiences, details about their neighborhood, readiness and reasons for adopting, and references.

There were 40 pages of legalese I had signed off on. Where on earth was the Home Study? Surely, I had missed it while scouring through the pile of paperwork. I frantically searched again. Then I ran to a neighbor to ask her to translate all the legal jargon in the adoption statute. It was the weekend; there was no one to call to get clarification, and my appointment with my own lawyer wasn't until the following Friday.

I knew I could not let go of Lynn, but how would I live with the finality of the adoption if I couldn't legally get him back? I fantasized again about Angela bringing him to me and telling me she understood now and agreed that Lynn should be with me, saying: "Samantha, I'm sorry. Forgive me for not understanding. Thank you for trying. I love you." Had I lost my marbles?

Do I Have Any Legal Recourse?

I found myself determined to discover a way; maybe there truly was a loophole that would help me get my son back. The ongoing internal tug of war seemed like walking on a treadmill with the brakes on.

Behind the scenes of pretending to be okay, I nervously waited for the meeting with my lawyer. From her I would learn whether or not I had any recourse in the matter. I chewed off all my fingernails during the many times I read and reread all the paperwork. My family loaned me $7,000 to help with legal costs.

I was open to a way to do joint custody if need be, but Angela had refused my earlier suggestion that we resolve things that way.

In the 1980s, "Baby M's" mother had won visitation rights in her historical case. Could I at least get that? From the sidelines, my family became my allies. They had all but abandoned me on my pregnancy journeys and during the time I had given Lynn up, but now they were calling constantly, checking in, and were rooting for me to claim my motherhood.

It was a Saturday when I had received all the legal papers in the mail. The next day was Mother's Day. Was that a coincidence?

Pastor Harry, Can You Help Me?

During the Sunday service, where Harry was a pastor, he shared his own story. It was called: "A Tale of Two Mothers." His grandmother had raised him, but he admitted that more than anything what he really wanted was his own mother to care for him. While growing up, he had a recurring dream about her coming back. She showed up in his life when he turned 18; before that, his grandmother had banned his birth mother from his life because her history of alcoholism was full of too many broken promises and relapses.

Harry's talk drove me to tears. After the service, I asked if he could help me get my son back. His own mother had now been clean and sober for some time, and they had a good relationship, while full of regrets for the time they had missed. Harry didn't want to see the same fate for me and said, "Of course, Samantha, I will help you."

The following day, we went to the adoption support group together to see if they might be able to give me more clarity about the law. There were seven people in the circle, mostly adoptees in the midst of searching for their biological parents. A sympathetic birthmom was there. She was much further along in the grieving process but, even after five years, she hadn't recovered from her loss.

We could only guess what would happen in my case. I couldn't hang on to any expectation. I just had to wait and see what the lawyer would say.

Harry didn't tell me until later, but, at the time, he didn't think I would be able to get Lynn back. When I got home from the support group, I found the Home Study in the mail. I called Harry and sang, "Alleluia. The great storm is over. Lift up your wings and fly." I read him the statute I had received from the last meeting of the support group. If I was reading correctly, it said I had five additional days after the Home Study was delivered to revoke the adoption.

This was my last hope. In order to know if I had interpreted it right, I needed to wait for the appointment with my lawyer, which was not until that Friday, at the end of the business week—five days of hanging on the cliff's edge.

Preparing a Nest

Meanwhile, no matter what happened, I had already been preparing to move away from my new house. I knew I could not stand living only two blocks from my son, not knowing when I might see him again on an outing with Angela. Vanna had offered me her small studio apartment in town where she only stayed occasionally anyway. It was conveniently next to Ralph's house.

I still struggled to get out of bed in the morning, let alone move households, so my birth team, fully aware (except for Angela) of what was brewing, helped with the move. Additionally, Vanna and Harry said they would help me find a renter for my house. Peter lived in one of the houses next door to Ralph but was being careful not to get too involved. I would take whatever help I could get from him. What would I have done without my friends?

On Friday, the morning of the fifth day of waiting for a meeting with my lawyer, I went to meet Harry so that he could accompany me. As I approached Harry's office, I looked down and saw a four-leaf clover growing right outside his door. I picked it, and stood in the sunshine praying, hoping. When he opened his door, I held it up to him and said, "This is my answer. Now I know I'll be able to get Lynn back."

Telling Angela the Hard Truth

The lawyer told me I had done my homework and I could take the paperwork she was giving me to show Angela and then take my son home. Wow! I was shaking. I took some deep breaths, wiped away a flood of tears, and felt deep relief. There was no contest.

Although I believed I was now following the best of all outcomes for Lynn, I was scared to death to call Angela. When I did, I said we needed to talk in person. She said she did not have time and I should just tell her whatever I needed to say.

So, I blurted it out, "Angela, I'm afraid to tell you. I have struggled too long trying to adjust to our adoption plan and can't live with it. I discovered that I still have a chance to revoke the agreement and that is what I've decided to do."

I heard a click, and we were suddenly disconnected. Then I called Ralph to let him know what was happening, and we agreed to call each other as soon as we found out anything. Over the next few hours, I couldn't get through to Angela by phone. Finally, a neighbor's voice answered for her and said she would be the go-between and would call me back soon.

Homecoming!

While the afternoon was wearing on, Harry sat with me holding my hand and listened to me make phone calls to family and friends—excitedly sharing my belated "birth announcement." Then Ralph called to catch us up on how things were playing out. He said Angela had called and asked him about my crazy actions. She had asked, "Aren't you concerned?" He didn't go into it and just told her he was supporting my choice. As a result, she realized she couldn't consider suing for custody. Maybe she wanted to sue me because of witnessing my erratic behavior in order to protect Lynn from an unstable mother. She was in love with him, of course, and it was true that I was depleted, but I wasn't crazy. I didn't know how long it would take to get myself put back together, but I knew this was the right thing to do.

I had limited time to deliver the paperwork to Angela, but she refused to see me. I told her go-between neighbor that Harry would deliver it. Angela didn't want to see him either, so one of his colleagues delivered the papers for me. Once she received the paperwork, she accepted the inevitable; she had no choice and asked for a few days more with Lynn to say goodbye.

That brief interlude bought me time to get more settled into my new space at Vanna's apartment. And then, as if by magic, Lynn was returned to me; Harry delivered him into my arms. It had been two and a half months of sheer terror separating from my son.

I hugged Lynn tight, smelled him, kissed him again and again, looked into his eyes, rocked him; it was a homecoming moment never to be forgotten. I called my parents to share the news and wish my dad a happy birthday. "Samantha, this news is the best birthday present I ever received. Thank you. I love you."

Ralph, Peter, Vanna, Christine, and Liam showed up for the reunion. Lynn smiled, cooed, and played with his tongue, while meeting the eyes of this jubilant cheerleading team once again. He was home for good, with his forever original family.

Angela would not see me, and I was asked not to call her.

Still thinking Lynn would be visiting her though, she sent a note asking me to send him back with the special blanket he had received from his adoptive grandparents and extra cloth diapers. I could drop him off with a neighbor who would then deliver Lynn to her. The negative feelings toward me didn't bode well for my baby's future. I decided that if Angela couldn't meet me directly, I was not going to have her stay in touch with Lynn. I didn't want him to have to absorb the bad energy between us. I couldn't tell her directly, so I said a prayer for Angela concluding with: "I'm sorry Angela; Please forgive me. Thank you. I love you."

7
Is There a Light at the End of the Tunnel?

I HADN'T PAID ATTENTION to much information about the aftermath of birthing a child, in part because I'd never planned to play the "mom" role. Besides, I thought I knew enough about parenting after helping to raise so many younger siblings and didn't want to ever have that job again.

Now I was asking, "How is it that parenthood is approached with such nonchalance? Might it help if we were somehow forewarned, knowing that even if everything went right, we would still have enormous adjustments to make?" It seems that people muddle along in the process of procreation and then, as things unfold, they/we roll with the punches as best we can.

I had learned the basics of *pregnancy* during the nine-month gestation process, merely by following the protocol of doctor visits and taking some childbirth classes with Angela and Peter. But that did not prepare me/us to be *parents*. My situation had additional layers to sort through. Certainly nothing had prepared me for the bind I still found myself in.

Atypical Parenting Initiation

I was happy to have a friend tell me about a project she was working on that would help set up systems to provide support for the "fourth trimester." She explained that that is the three-month time period after the baby is born, a time which is usually overlooked, both regarding the baby's overwhelming experience and the mother's postpartum journey. I was invited to one of their planning meetings and asked to give feedback. Mine was not a typical situation by any means, but there are plenty of unique situations that benefit from a supportive intervention. I felt acknowledged and validated by that group.

I was looking at life going forward but also reviewing the totality of the initiation to parenthood, expanding my thoughts to include the time *before* making babies. Wouldn't it be great if we humans knew from the get-go about how to navigate and provide healthy parenting, *starting* with being a healthy person ourselves? This knowledge could contribute positively to each child's outcome for their mental health and wellbeing; it could influence their development during preconception, time in utero and after being born, etc. ultimately creating a functional society. Playing games with my mind by entertaining an ideal world was one way to escape my current turmoil.

Parenting brings up our own emotions from being parented. I was realizing the impact of how my own subconscious feelings around abandonment had informed my design and choice in almost abandoning my own child. Now that I was triggered by past wounds, I would need guidance in processing them.

Certainly, there are no guarantees that come with this everyday risk-taking phenomenon that has populated the planet. With all the variation on how things can play out, one best be able to embrace the unknown and the mystery as part of being human. I was just exasperated by the overwhelm for each and every one that tread these waters, feeling great compassion and empathy, including for myself in the moment. My initiation to parenthood, with its unique twists, took me on an unpredictable roller coaster ride.

Lynn's uncomplicated natural birth and recovery time at the hospital had enabled me to quickly forget the pain of childbirth.

Before he was born, I'd been somewhat prepared for physical pain and had practiced breathing exercises that might help me manage it. If things didn't go as we imagined, I knew there were back up options to choose from, come what may. More painful than the birthing process was finding myself catapulted into an aftershock of disabling emotions from an extremely confusing and complex set of changing outcomes. From the outside I looked pretty normal. What people couldn't see or understand was the hell I was going through on the inside.

I had sweated the five unsettling days awaiting my lawyer's endorsement to revoke the adoption but anticipated the good news that I was about to truly be Lynn's legal mom again, in the fullest sense. When the lawyer confirmed the rights to my child, excited as I was, I also had to quickly face the reality of life with an infant, let alone life as an infant's single mom.

Most women spend nine months of pregnancy reorganizing their lives and preparing for motherhood. I had missed that part, and so getting Lynn back meant scrambling to make up for lost time. Many women also had the advantage of sharing the 24/7 load with a partner living in the same home. No matter. A mother's love rises to challenges.

As soon as Lynn was finally delivered into my arms again, I felt my broken heart begin to heal. Getting Lynn back changed my life forever. It was a second birthing of sorts, minus the physical pain, and so began the natural bonding of a reunited mother and child. I was hopelessly in love and, for the first time, committed to another person forever.

Healing the Severed Bond

My almost two-and-a-half-month-old son and I both had to readjust to our new, surreal reality. Though I had decided to finally honor my heart, something had been lost in the process.

Lynn initially did not make eye contact with me. How had this trauma impacted him?

I called Nancy Verrier to give her the news of the reunion, share some of the heavy feelings I still had, and ask her about the strange, almost-vacant look in Lynn's eyes, which rarely seemed to focus on me. She told me my son was likely unconsciously mad at me, that he didn't trust me, and that it would take time to heal the broken bond.

I had read somewhere that babies were resilient and bounced back, but then I learned that it wasn't that easy. Babies have cellular memory, with no words to describe their feelings.

Nancy advised me to stay at home until Lynn was at least 18 months old, in order to re-establish our bond. I learned that around that age babies grow beyond what experts call *object permanence*. Before that time, when anyone leaves a room, they aren't aware that the person will come back. That's why the game *peek-a-boo* is a surprise; they are first scared when their parent leaves the room, then a little shocked when they show up. It's not really a fun game for them. Lynn needed to learn to trust me again and know he was safe with me.

On top of a baby's normal issues in adjusting to this brand new world, Lynn's premature separation from me created an insecure attachment. Any added insecurity could trigger that trauma and re-open the wound.

It was strongly recommended that I be Lynn's main caretaker as much as possible and try to re-establish my milk flow. Also, from what I was reading, I learned that sharing a family bed helps maintain the natural bonding process, so he slept with me at night rather than being put in a crib in a dark room alone. It felt a little late in the game to get started, but I was determined to make up for lost time.

I sought guidance from a breastfeeding center to see if I could get my milk to flow again. From so many sleepless nights, a loss of appetite, and all the stress, I had lost weight and my body was worn out, but I would try anything to reconnect with my baby. The staff hooked me up to an apparatus that had a pouch to hold milk and showed me how to use it while Lynn squirmed hungrily on my lap. I went home with the gadgetry strapped to my chest, filled a pouch with nature's formula, and answered Lynn's demands for more. There were tubes attached to my nipples that would deliver the formula to Lynn as he suckled. Supposedly, the stimulation would cause my body to lactate again but after several weeks of trying, still feeling exhausted and with growing discouragement, I finally gave up. Lynn went along with whatever way I fed him. He had been a champion breast feeder, learned this new method of getting fed, and then transitioned easily into bottle feeding.

In those early months Lynn slept a lot and woke up seemingly content. I remember him crying only sometimes- maybe when he was in the middle of a diaper change and when he was hungry. His sucking sounds, lip smacking, cooing, oohs and aahs were music to my soul.

Postpartum Malaise on Steroids

Despite the sweet baby serenade and thinking my post-partum hell would magically and finally lift, the debilitation hung on instead, clouding the joy I might feel in mothering my son. I continued to wake up each morning with dry heaves, something that had started just after we separated. My only motivation to even get up at all was to care for Lynn. I had to believe this lingering and distressing time would end and that I would adapt.

My process included letting go of my project in Belize, and letting go of Peter and of single friends who couldn't relate to my new lifestyle. I also had to stop living in the past and beating myself up. I had no time or umph to socialize, something that had given me much pleasure, enjoyment, and support before Lynn's birth.

My family was delighted that I revoked the adoption, which showed in their frequent phone calls and letters, but they lived too far away to offer the kind of assistance I needed.

I was not being patient with my annoying emotions. The feelings of sadness, confusion, depression, and carrying intense fatigue all seemed interminable. Instead of the relief from suffering I had anticipated, every day I woke up feeling mentally, physically, emotionally, and spiritually bankrupt. With little daily support, I still pushed on.

Blessing Way

It was time to formally welcome Lynn into my circle of friends. On a perfect summer day at the ecovillage, we gathered for a Blessing Way celebration at a ceremonial circle in the woods, sitting on carved out tree stumps and creating a bubble of magic surrounding my baby boy. Lynn was welcomed into the world in the most beautiful, honoring way I had ever witnessed.

Ralph opened by reciting Kahlil Gibran's poem:

On Children [6]

Your children are not your children.
They are the sons and daughters of Life's longing for itself.
They come through you but not from you,
And though they are with you yet they belong not to you.
You may give them your love but not your thoughts,
For they have their own thoughts.
You may house their bodies but not their souls,
For their souls dwell in the house of tomorrow,
which you cannot visit, even in your dreams.
You may strive to be like them but seek not to make them like you.
For life goes not backward nor tarries with yesterday.

One by one, Lynn was gently passed around to all of his new friends, each taking their own time to be with him, the prince of the day. They recited more poetry, sang songs, danced with him, spoke wishes to him, whispered in his ear, and gave him sentimental gifts. At the end of the celebration, we planted his placenta under a serviceberry tree that would blossom each year around his birthday.

Recently a friend shared a recollection from that gathering—a story about a butterfly that landed on Lynn's finger. She said that time seemed to stop as Lynn and the butterfly stared into each other's eyes, having their own private conversation, maybe trading secrets. It seemed like a beautiful symbol for our experience—Lynn

---

[6] Gibran, Kahlil. From *The Prophet* (Knopf, 1923).

coming out of his cocoon into the mysterious world full of nectar. At the end of the day, I built a small fire and burned all the adoption papers I had signed. Despite the fanfare, I was like a zombie on the drive home.

My Lifeline: Family and Friends

My friend Catherine who had driven 500 miles for the blessing stayed on to help for a few days. Then my mother flew in for a weekend with several of my sisters. They all loved meeting and helping care for Lynn. By the end of the weekend, though, they all were feeling pretty helpless, needing to leave me in my depleted state. My mother asked if I would come home to Maine and let her help me take care of Lynn so that I could get some deep rest. I tried to reassure her that I would be better tomorrow, but soon my optimism soured into bitter reality.

Every tomorrow remained a nightmare I thought would never end. A group of friends bought me more weeks of a home delivery cloth diaper service and stocked my fridge with some healthy prepared meals. Harry got us out of the house for some beautiful drives and picnics in the mountains. Liam popped in a few times a week to play his train whistle, sing us tribal songs, and play with Lynn while I napped. Vanna and Christine checked in on me regularly. Christine's dog, Beau, accompanied her and plastered us with slobbery kisses. Several times a week, Ralph took his son out and gave me a break. Everyone tolerated my "dead battery" demeanor, my frozen inaction. I waited impatiently for time to heal.

With all this love, and with the opportunity to take time off work, I didn't need to leave the house much. Even if I couldn't feel it, it was a luxury to be able to manage Lynn's routine of feeding, diaper changes, walks, and other daily baby and home maintenance, without the pressure of working. I could go through the motions despite messed up emotions.

I continued to despair about ever getting my life back. Something seemed terribly wrong. My friends continued to hang in there with me as best they could. They were my lifelines in this troubled time.

When my sister Jane flew in for a visit, it didn't take her long to tire of my negative litany. She wanted me to do a therapeutic exercise, which I resisted at first; I was to make a list of ten possibilities for my future and then set them in motion. I told her nothing was possible. She persisted, and finally convinced me to write down a list of things that I might fantasize as possibilities. I laboriously came up with a list to please her, but

I didn't want to look at it again.

Cures for the Baby Blues

Visits to the doctor for Lynn, and for me, showed we were physically healthy. Lynn's development fit the graphs, and I was told the postpartum depression would eventually lift. My doctor couldn't give me a magic pill other than recommending an anti-depressant and sleeping pills. I feared medications would only make me dependent on them. My father, who had suffered from PTSD after WW II, had been on strong medications for his intractable depression. Those pills seemed to make a zombie out of him. Could I end up like that? We were gardeners. We helped build our own houses and now this? No, I decided, I wasn't going to follow the doctor's protocol.

Even though I wanted to stay alive and be a good mother to Lynn, I often wished I could die to escape feeling such intense shame and emptiness. Would death give me that freedom? I went to therapy for several months, but when I learned that my therapist had worked at an adoption agency placing babies and had never bore a child herself,

I no longer trusted that she understood my perspective. I had to stop seeing her.

My health insurance plan ran out six months after Lynn's birth, but it had never covered the alternative treatments I was interested in anyway. Since I didn't trust many of Western medicine's prescriptions, I used my savings to work with various alternative health practitioners, hoping they might have something to get me healed. I had acupuncture, Reiki and massage. I took herbs, visited psychics, and was blessed with water from the seven major rivers of the world.

I began mixing a spiritual quest into the search for healing. I visited an array of Christian churches, read the Bible, witnessed people speaking in tongues, and had an exorcist try to remove my demons. When none of this worked, I moved on to read passages from the world's wisdom teachings. I zeroed in on a correspondence course with the Self Realization Fellowship that taught eastern philosophy and practices including guidance in meditation. This helped some, bringing the suffering down a notch, but I needed time to integrate the practice, and I was already at the end of my rope.

Despite all my attempts to find a magic bullet, everything I tried seemed either fruitless or it would take too long to take effect. Impatient for results, I jumped from one healing path to another. Each, in their own way though, served to etch away at the layers of disease my life had accumulated.

One Day at a Time

I had hit bottom and could find no way out of that dungeon. Friends became tired of my unrelenting, hopeless discourse. They had busy lives and visited less and less. I lived on instant meals and fast food, feeling more and more alone. I described my bodily reality as similar to having a flu that never went away. Lori, a sympathetic neighbor, gave me a homeopathic remedy that for a few days had a magical effect, lifting me out of the depression. It brought a glimmer of hope! Then I fell back into the same despair. Although I was able to keep up a consistent routine of baby care, I often spent the time while Lynn was asleep desperately trying to figure out why I was not bouncing back and what to do next.

When Lynn woke up, I would often turn on soft music and dance with him, even if I tired quickly. He was thriving and would coo and smile no matter what was going on with me. How could life be so dark with this little soul lighting up the room? Lynn was sleeping through the night, but I was restless. After each night of sleeplessness, I hated getting up to face the same desperate reality.

Vanna was living at the ecovillage, too far to drive over, and anyway, she felt helpless seeing me suffer. It only made her think about her own unknown birthmom. Peter was nowhere to be seen. Even though I knew he was next door, he might as well have been in Timbuktu. Before I chose motherhood, I had dozens of friends who shared my joys. Now my new routine and the relentless suffering seemed to drive everyone away from me—everyone but my baby.

Whenever I picked Lynn up and rocked him, it felt like some sweet, strong spirit was holding me, too. "You're worth every minute," I would whisper. "You're beautiful. I love you to the moon and back." His hand would be wrapped around my thumb as he fell asleep cooing. And then the pall of darkness would fall over me again.

I'll Adopt You Both

When I could take no more, my theatrical friend Christine showed up for a visit with her dog, Beau. He sat beside me, his puppy dog eyes expressing sympathy for me. I said, "I wish when people wanted to adopt, they would adopt the whole family, making sure everyone was okay, and if not, then they should find a way to share the burden somehow. I know I can't live without my baby, but *he* needs a healthier mom."

"I'll adopt you both," said Christine matter-of-factly. She gave me a questioning puppy dog look and then her face broke into a radiant smile. "It will be win-win. I always wanted a family, and Beau would love it too."

Whenever Christine came over, she would hold Lynn and he would grab at her curly hair and pull, then squeal with excitement as she shook her head, and pursed her lips and made silly faces. She gave him baths, playing splashing games, both of them laughing up a storm. They went on fun walks, with Beau sometimes helping to pull the stroller. Her invitation for us to move in with her seemed like a great alternative to endless days of feeling sick and alone. With a glimmer of hope, I packed my bags.

On my last day in Vanna's apartment, she popped in with George, her sock monkey extraordinaire. She said Lynn needed a friend, and I needed George's magic. She told me he was maintenance-free, so we adopted him.

"Thank you, Vanna. I'm sorry you had to move for us. Please forgive me. Now you can have your house back. I love you."

Living with Christine gave me much-needed relief from the effort of daily survival. As I was still running on empty, Christine let me lean on her. She gave Lynn some good, sweet, "auntie" attention. I did get out some, but mostly to get groceries. In search of some additional support, I began taking Lynn to a playgroup for moms and babies a few times a week.

In meeting other new moms, I was surprised to learn more about their experiences. Their situations seemed to be what I secretly yearned for, but in comparing stories, I got a reality check. I found out that most of them had varying degrees of post-partum depression. It gave me something to relate with and made me feel less alone.

Our new home, with Christine's support was a perfect place to land. It relieved some of the stress of single mothering. As time went on, though, even after several more months of convalescence, I felt miserable. I simply was unable to drag myself out of bed for any length of time. I began to wonder if I'd been caught in some kind of unrelenting hellish possession. Thoughts of suicide came to me often. What kind of mother could I be for Lynn to grow up with if I never got better? I was uncomfortable in my body every moment of the day, from the minute I woke up with dry heaves, and while forcing myself to walk through the day in a fog, carrying extreme fatigue, hopelessness, and misery. Same train wreck, different day.

I'll Quit Smoking If You Come Home

Out of the blue one day, my dad, who had caught wind of me talking suicide, called me on the phone. He *never* called me or anyone on the phone.

"Hello?"

"Samantha, it's your dad."

"Dad? You are calling me?!"

"Yes, I heard you've been struggling. I want to see you and meet Lynn. I'm calling to ask if you will come home so your mom can help you."

"I've been so sick, Dad; I just want to die."

"Samantha, I've been there. Believe me: those feelings will pass."

Silence.

"Honey, if you come home, I promise you that I'll quit smoking."

That was when I started crying. When I was ten years old, I'd tried to get him to quit smoking, telling him I'd stop eating until he did. I actually ate nothing for an entire day. Then he told me that his cigarettes were like nails. He was pounding them into his heart, hoping someday it would stop. It sounded so morbidly pathetic, as though he didn't even care about life. I stopped trying to get him to quit after that.

Now I said, "Really, Dad? If you really promise, then I will come home."

"Let me know when I can pick you up at the Truckstop," he chuckled.

"Thank you, Dad. I'm sorry. Please forgive me, and I love you. I'll be home soon."

It took every ounce of energy I had to organize the trip and get ready to go. My brother Paul drove all the way down from Maine to help me with the move. I put things in storage and filled my car with essentials, not knowing when I would be back.

As a small token of my gratitude for Christine, I gave her a special theatrical mask called "the Jester" that I'd gotten in Italy, something of mine that she had admired. She told me she would be there for me when I needed to return.

"Thank you, Christine, I'm sorry, please forgive me, and I love you."

I caravanned, following my brother back to Maine. "Thank you, Paul. I'm sorry for the hassle; please forgive me, and I love you."

Being in my home state with my parents' support, for however long, was a useful, temporary distraction. At least I didn't have to pretend I was okay. I could fall apart and not be embarrassed for feeling so miserable.

Within an hour of getting home, I sat with my dad while he smoked his last cigarette. His decision to stop smoking was a dream come true, even though he already had lung cancer. I never knew how much he cared about me. He never knew how to show it, but apparently, he remembered what had been so important to me when I was a child. That meant the world to me.

My mom loved caring for Lynn. Many of my siblings brought their children, Lynn's cousins, for frequent visits. He was held, read to, sung to, danced with and entertained with all kinds of play. Ah the gift of a large family!

Infant Toddler Sign Language

I was starting to teach Lynn sign language, a great communication tool for babies. They hear things repeatedly and often have receptive language; be careful what you say, but they can't talk back! Because their motor development is ahead of their verbal development, until around 18 months old, there is a window of opportunity to teach them sign language. Just like hearing things over and over while learning to talk, they need to see the signs repeatedly to learn them. A good example of this is when babies sign "bye-bye," the parents go gaga over this. It has been found that hearing children of Deaf parents can sign their first signs around eight months old. Longitudinal studies have shown that hearing babies who learned some sign language, learn English faster.

Dark Night of the Soul, Ad Nauseam

I went through tests at my family doctor's office. They showed nothing that might explain my lingering fatigue, so the chronic fatigue syndrome label got slapped on as a diagnosis.

I was advised to get shock treatment and even visited a clinic to explore that option. While I sat in the waiting room, I talked with patients who had already been through shock therapy. They told some scary stories about their short-lived improvements. They seemed to have gone through a revolving door, returning sometimes yearly for a tune up. By the time I was called for my interview, I felt guarded and afraid. They told me I was asking too many personal questions of the other patients. We agreed this treatment was not for me.

In my misery, I caved in and accepted the other suggested protocol: anti-depressants. But I got a prescription for medicines I never took. Instead, I started saving those pills, imagining and plotting how I could do myself in. The supposed diagnosis of chronic fatigue sounded like a death sentence to me. I certainly did not want to put my son through years of living with a mom who couldn't take care of him properly.

I'd no idea life would turn out like this when I revoked the adoption. Should I have left Lynn with the family that had wanted to adopt him instead of dragging him through my hell?

It was too late to give him back now, so I *had* to pull myself together. I wondered what effect this was having on Lynn.

My mother took care of Lynn with doting love while I struggled to survive. Staying with my parents felt like a safe harbor at first but, after several months, I began to feel more stressed. Although Lynn didn't seem to be impacted by others' realities as long as he was fed and held lovingly, I was highly sensitive to others' struggles.

My dad's condition was especially hard on me. He was dealing with both PTSD flashbacks and lung cancer. He had very little energy and no will to live. Lynn could bring a sparkle to my dad's eyes when I sat him on Grandpa's lap, but Grandpa ran out of energy quickly.

It was depressing to see my dad in such poor health, and it triggered my own despair. The daily train whistle could still perk me up for a moment, but then, as soon as that sound faded, I too would fade back into darkness.

It was a long winter. How apropos—the season of my dark night of the soul. There were moments when the light peeked in, usually when I witnessed Lynn's fresh view of the world. The day I took him outdoors to introduce him to snow, he was mesmerized by the thick white flakes as they fell. Then, back inside, I gave him his first taste of hot chocolate. He signed "more" to grandma, a word he knew we understood. Then grandma gave him a nice warm bath in the kitchen sink. He was in good hands, and we were safe, living in a holding pattern until my body recovered.

Where, oh where was the proverbial light at the end of this tunnel? Or was that just another train coming at me head-on?

I took out my quote collection and read Rumi:

The Tavern [7]

All day I think about it, then at night I say it.
Where did I come from, and what am I
suppose to be doing?
I have no idea.
My soul is from elsewhere, I'm sure of that.
And I intend to end up there.
This drunkenness began in some other tavern.

---

[7] Barks, Coleman. *The Essential Rumi* (Castle Books, 1995).

When I get back to that place,
I'll be completely sober, Meanwhile
I'm like a bird from another continent,
Sitting in this aviary.
The day is coming when I fly off,
But who is it now in my ear who hears my voice?
Who says words without my mouth?

Who looks out with my eyes?
What is the soul? I cannot stop asking.

...If I could taste one sip of an answer,
I could break out of this prison for drunks.
I didn't come here of my own accord,
And I can't leave that way.
Whoever brought me here will have to
Take me home.

8
Do You Believe in Miracles?

OVER THE NEXT FEW MONTHS, I tried a variety of living situations that I hoped would get me through until I was in better shape. Unfortunately, I didn't feel comfortable anywhere I landed.

My brother Michael, who lived with his wife and three children under the ages of four, generously and kindly offered us a place to stay. They were extremely busy parents, both holding down jobs with long hours. I thought I might be able to help out. Sadly, in only a few weeks' time I completely ran out of the little energy I had. Feeling that I had nothing to offer them and seeing myself as an added burden who wasn't even able to offer childcare without resorting to TV to entertain the kids, I started looking for another alternative. Instead of enjoying the time I'd been given to help in mothering this fun pack of little ones, I felt that my focus should be on Lynn, and on getting myself better, even if I didn't yet know how.

While I was figuring out where to go next, my family gathered at a local pizza parlor to celebrate Lynn's first birthday. They all fussed over him and commented on what a happy baby he was. Holding onto the table legs, he danced to the jukebox music. If he tried to clap or take a step, he would fall, then laugh, and then pull himself up to start over again. When asked how I got such a perfect baby, I'd say that I'd paid a high price, but he was worth every bit of it!

We then received an offer to stay with my twin, Noreen, and her family. They had a large, comfortable house. With her four children away at school all day, there would be lots of quiet time. This arrangement bought me more time on my road to recovery even though I didn't notice any improvement. In the evening, Lynn reveled in all the playtime with his cousins. It didn't take long, though, for me to start feeling guilty about intruding on their family, worrying about how long it would take for me to get better. Although Lynn adapted quickly and was comfortable no matter where we stayed, I was tired of moving from place to place. I felt restless and unable to commit to any other offers from family. I needed to take Lynn home to see and be with his dad.

Suicidal Ideation

While we were still in Maine, I went to see a highly recommended chiropractor who practiced kinesiology. He diagnosed me with a chronic gluten intolerance. He was the first practitioner who ever asked me what I ate. He suspected that intolerance to gluten was the link to my depleted energy. He also suspected a link to my depleted state could be an Epstein-Barr recurrence; something that could show up any time when I went through life stressors and could easily be misdiagnosed as a mental health issue. The muscle testing he did seemed a little like hocus pocus, but I was willing to try anything. I followed his advice and started eating whole organic foods, all without gluten.

My quotation collection gave me some temporary distraction, but the words too were losing their influence. Over and over again I read Rumi:

Make me sweet again,

And fresh

and fragrant

and grateful for any small event.

I was only going through the motions though, not trusting I would get any relief. More often, it seemed it might be time for me to leave the planet. I could take only so much of this black hole of depression, lacking energy to get through a day.

With no relief in sight, I fantasized various ways to end my life. If I did it in Maine, for example, it would be easy to go down to the sea, walk along a jetty's slippery rocks, and then let myself fall into the water, hitting my head on the rocks as I fell. Since there was often at least one person walking or running on the packed, wet sand along the shore, however, I'd probably be found before I was dead. No, that wouldn't work.

Only my love for Lynn kept me alive through these dark months, and I knew it. Still, I wasn't going to be dependent on this baby for my own wellbeing. I also believed that Lynn needed time to be with his father and, since I remained hopelessly locked into my depression no matter where I was, I decided that Lynn and I would return to the Shenandoah Valley.

When I spoke to Ralph, he was patient and supportive of my process. I didn't mention my suicidal thoughts. I intended to return Lynn safely to his dad and then bow out. I had saved enough pills to do the job. Mixed with alcohol, I had no doubt they'd kill me.

I said my farewells to my family, thinking I would never see them again. I felt hollow inside, feeling nothing at all, not even remorse for plotting my own demise. I was truly at my wit's end. No amount of baby cooing was going to bring me back.

"Thank you, my beloved family. I'm sorry. Please forgive me. I love you."

Abracadabra!

On the drive back, as we moved southward, it was an experience of driving from a winter landscape into budding and blossoming trees, with greenery peeking through the meadows: Spring! Nearing the Shenandoah Mountains and just two hours from home, my life underwent a complete mystical change. Suddenly, out of nowhere, I went from feeling so heavily burdened that I might not make it back in one piece to feeling human once again as those dark feelings loosened their stranglehold on me, and my burden dissolved in a split second. In a flash. Just like that. Like magic. *Poof!*

Could I explain it? I could not. I knew *what* had happened, but I had no idea *how* it had occurred or *why*.

I pulled over and glanced back at my sleeping baby. Then I pinched my legs, my arms, my face, over and over again. I slapped my face to check if I was dreaming. I felt an inner lightness I had never experienced before. I had waited for this kind of elation all my life. The sticky ooze of my desperation had evaporated in the clean mountain air. What on God's green earth had *happened*?

As tears of relief overcame me, I drove on to a wayside rest area not far from where I had spent a hellish night almost a year earlier. I parked my car at the far end of the lot and sat staring back at Lynn. He was now awake, smiling, looking me in the eyes and saying "mum, mum, mum, mum." I felt like those thousand pieces of my broken heart had miraculously melded together. I smiled back, shaking my head in wonder. I lifted him out of his car seat and out of the car, hugging him and dancing circles around the parking lot, gazing into his eyes in disbelief, as he gazed into mine. I wanted to shout out loud to God, "Thank you! I'm sorry. Forgive me. I love you!"

Welcome Back!

When I got back to Ralph's neighborhood, he and Peter were waiting for us. Ralph reached out for Lynn and wrapped him into his arms rocking him from side to side. He was so happy to see him! Peter hugged me and then we pulled Ralph and Lynn in for a group hug. We hummed in unison, repeating it several times: "When Johhny Comes Marching Home Again. Hoorah! Hoorah!" I was back from the war!

Ralph had moved next door to share Peter's house so that Lynn and I had a comfortable place to land. Before I'd left Maine, Peter told me he was ready to be of more support to me than he'd been when I'd left several months earlier, although not in the sense a romance anymore, just a supportive friendship.

It was great to feel the vibrancy of life moving through me again! After the long drive back, having received a warm welcome, I sat down and sobbed with relief, free of the deadly feelings that had controlled me longer than I thought anyone could endure.

Christine then arrived, wearing the Jester mask I had gifted her, and shouted repeatedly while dancing around clapping, "Lynn and mommy are home!" then tightly embracing us. Beau joined in the jubilance, giving us the usual slobbery kisses. Then Liam, Vanna, and Harry arrived, delivering the warmth of deep friendship! We were home!

Feeling free of that interminable distress, I was finally ready to be a mom. Surely this was heaven on earth!

I pinched myself for days to see if any remnant of what had haunted me was still there. Being possessed with that dark loathsome drudgery seemed to be gone for good. In this new reality, I experienced the same kind of bliss I'd felt in a dream after a ritual ceremony in Belize a year before Lynn was born on a magical Spring Equinox.

During our first week back, I got hold of the train schedule and took Lynn to hear and watch the trains go by, that soothing familiar lullaby welcoming us home. It was almost summertime again, and all the daisies were in bloom.

One evening I picked up my favorite book of Rumi poems and read *The Guest House*,[8] words that resonated with me deeply:

> *This being human is a guest house.*
> *Every morning a new arrival.*
>
> *A joy, a depression, a meanness,*
> *some momentary awareness comes*
> *As an unexpected visitor.*
>
> *Welcome and entertain them all.*
> *Even if they're a crowd of sorrows,*
> *who violently sweep your house*
> *empty of its furniture,*
> *still treat each guest honorably.*
> *He may be clearing you out*
> *for some new delight.*

---

[8] Barks, Coleman. *The Essential Rumi* (Castle Books, 1995).

The dark thought, the shame, the malice,
meet them at the door laughing,
and invite them in.
Be grateful for whoever comes,
because each has been sent
as a guide from beyond.

9

Cleaning Up Train Wrecks

THERE WAS STILL SOME DEBRIS to clean up in the wake of the previous year's train wreck. Lynn and I were getting resettled, and I was deeply grateful to be feeling back to normal. I appreciated Ralph for waiting out the recovery time I'd spent for long months in Maine without ever demanding to see his son. It warmed my heart to see the connection he'd hoped for begin to blossom once again, and I knew how great it was for Lynn to have his dad present in person in his life.

Making Ends Meet

I needed to talk to Ralph about money. I had gone through most of my savings and my family had been very generous. My townhouse was rented out and had helped keep me afloat, but now I needed that rental income to pay rent elsewhere, on top of living expenses. It wasn't Ralph's fault that I had gotten him into this, and I felt guilty asking. So, I didn't ask him for an exorbitant amount—only what I needed to get by.

A few other friends moved in to live with us and shared in our household expenses. Phyllis, a founding member of the ecovillage where I had lived, always had wise insight on anything I was going through. She was knowledgeable about eastern teachings from masters, Osho and Adyashanti. While she was in transition waiting on the process of getting a house built at the ecovillage, we had the pleasure of living with her.

What Lynn loved about Phyllis was her introducing him to new foods—what an amazing cook! And a Deaf man new to town, Brian, joined our household. He taught ASL, including to Lynn, who benefited greatly from living in our bilingual household.

Family Constellations

At the ecovillage, I attended a Family Constellations workshop with a facilitator and twelve other participants. Over time, this unique healing modality helped me review parts of my family history. The workshop further helped release some entrenched feelings of abandonment and ultimately brought me great clarity, understanding and appreciation, especially for my parents. I could see where I had run away from relationships that smelled of commitment in my adult life to compensate for the burden I felt from having too much responsibility while growing up in a big family. Using that coping mechanism, I had even tried to abandon my own offspring! With the guidance I received, the pieces of my life began to make more sense. I felt I could forgive myself and everyone else. There was a new ease.

I was so grateful to have somehow miraculously become a stay-at-home mom, given my powerful allergic reaction to the idea. It was a healing journey to be on. I had torn down the walls of resistance to any commitment that might tie me down. I felt a renewed love for my family and a deep abiding love for my baby. I no longer lived the lie that I didn't need anyone and could do things myself. Maybe a romantic partnership too was possible.

Facing Angela

My biggest fear now was facing Angela, who had put her heart into the plan to be Lynn's adoptive mom. I thought I might run into her in a store and felt sad to imagine wanting to avoid her. I knew that ultimately neither of us wanted to be alienated from the other. Wanting to earn her friendship back, I called to see if she was available for mediation.

"Hello?"

"Hi, Angela. This is Samantha. Can we talk?"

I heard a deep breath, then, "Hi, Samantha." Then silence.

"I know it's hard to talk. I've been afraid to call," I said.

"I'm here Samantha. I just don't know what to say."

"Can we get a third person to help us talk to each other? I think we'll need some support in facing this, but I'm hoping we might come to some understanding and maybe even some resolution."

After another long pause, she said, "Well, maybe...Okay. Let's try to find a time."

"I so appreciate your being available for this, Angela." My voice quivered. "My friend Pastor Harry offered to sit with us. You can bring someone you are comfortable with, if you'd like. How about I call you back after I get his schedule, okay?"

"Thanks for taking the first step, Samantha. I'll talk to you soon."

We hung up and I breathed a sigh of relief. It seemed easier than I'd expected. Perhaps we both were ready.

We arranged to meet with Harry at his office. I brought daffodils for everyone. I expected Angela to be full of judgments, anger and a sense of being wronged. Most of what I was feeling was just plain fear. It turned out we were both genuinely sad about what had happened to our idealistic plans. Each of us was also willing to hear the other's story with an open heart.

We talked about the paths we had taken in the last year since we had actually shared time together-the time I called to revoke the adoption. After getting over that hurdle in our conversation, sharing tears from those difficult memories, we felt more at ease as our friendship was being repaired. There was much to catch up on.

I learned that Angela had searched for and found an agency that would allow her to adopt an infant even though she was single. She was currently awaiting her turn to adopt a foreign-born child. It could take a year. This time, however, there would be no birth-mother hovering in the wings (and slowly losing her mind, if that was the case).

I told Angela about my time in Maine: the horrible guilt I'd felt, the suffering that had harrowed my heart and mind and left me almost unable to function. I also shared the strange elation that had so suddenly freed me of that misery in a single, magical moment I still didn't understand but would always be grateful for.

We agreed to meet again soon, this time for her to reunite with Lynn. We were both thankful for Harry's careful and respectful guidance, which contributed to our coming to an understanding of what had happened to each of us. The reconnection was a huge relief and very heartwarming!

Two days later we met up in a park. Angela took a long look at Lynn, lifted him in her arms, and said, "I remember you." I was touched to witness this reconnection. Then she asked to sit alone with him for a bit, so I left him in her arms and walked far enough away to give them some space.

I saw how Lynn seemed to respond to Angela right away. There could be heard lots of babbling and giggling. My heart overflowed with appreciation for her willingness to find a place of forgiveness so that we could begin to rebuild our friendship.

Soon after Angela and I had reconnected, her parents asked for a reunion and to bring Lynn. They took us out to eat and I told them, "In my heart you will always be Lynn's grandparents."

(I'm jumping ahead because I can't wait to share that later down the road, when Lynn was two years old, Angela adopted a daughter from a town in Belize, not far from where I'd spent a college semester. Her daughter Crystal was a beautiful, brown-eyed child with straight black hair and a captivating smile. She was just a year younger than Lynn. When seeing her in Angela's arms the first time, I finally felt the last vestiges of my guilt melt away.)

We Love You All!

As life settled into more of a normal rhythm, the one sad development was that Harry decided to move away so he'd be closer to his daughter and granddaughter. He had been such a rock of support, so instrumental in providing both guidance and mediation, and he'd gone full circle with us. Was his job done? We were all sad to say goodbye.

"Thank you, Harry. I'm sorry. Please forgive me. I love you."

I rekindled many of my deep friendships, especially with those who went through my tough start with motherhood.

"Thank you, friends. I'm sorry for how hard it was for you to support me. Please forgive me. I love you."

Everything is Possible for Samantha and Lynn

One day while organizing my file cabinet I happened upon the list my sister Jane had asked me to create when Lynn was only a few months old. It made no sense, as everything on it seemed impossible. But, despite the train wreck, less than a year later, ten out of the eleven possibilities had happened.

I had written:

1. *Miraculous healing of mind, body and soul.*

2. *Samantha has embraced motherhood and envisions a lifetime of comfort in her role.*
3. *A complete and miraculous healing between Samantha and Angela, and Angela's family, has occurred.*
4. *Samantha and Lynn are living close to Ralph and have planted roots. Daffodils are in bloom.*
5. *Samantha's connection to the rural ecovillage is intact, despite the move to town.*
6. *Work in the Deaf community continues to be a strong passion.*
7. *Marriage is being proposed and is likely to occur soon.*
8. *Samantha and Lynn are financially healthy and secure.*
9. *Lynn's relationship with daddy Ralph is comfortable and workable for Lynn, Samantha, Ralph (and his partner).*
10. *Lynn is healthy and has strong, supportive care.*
11. *God and the angels are ever-present and fully aware and strengthening Samantha and Lynn.*

I scratched out number 7 which read, "Marriage is being proposed and is likely to occur soon." and wrote: "Marriage to life has occurred." Perhaps someday the other kind of marriage would happen in my life.

Daffodils were in bloom. The sound of Liam's voice echoed in my ear: "We give thanks to the rising sun, and to the flowers and trees…"

Part II
Fall 1963 – Winter 1996

Kyra Peregrine, artist

"There was an old woman who lived in a shoe. She had so many children she didn't know what to do."

—*Mother Goose*

10
Adopt Them All

"THERE'S 16 CHILDREN in your family?" My high school sociology teacher shouted in disbelief, echoing years of other voices stupefied by such a large number.

It was all I'd ever known. Introductions on the first day of school were always hard. The idea of one coming from such a huge family gave other students plenty of fodder for strong reactions—some of them coming up with creative, often hurtful jokes. Friends sometimes asked me to name all my brothers and sisters. I could rattle our names off in one breath: "EarlMarieAnthonySueSamanthaNoreenSharonJaneMargaretJoanPaulLizKayScottMichaelChris."

It was almost like saying supercalifragilisticexpialidocious. On the first day of school, I would try to get by saying I had one brother and a twin sister.

"A twin?" some would ask. "You're so lucky."

But then the teacher might ask, "Isn't Earl your older brother, and what about Anthony, and don't you have a bunch of sisters?" On my brother Michael's first day of kindergarten, when they asked how many brothers and sisters he had, he didn't know. He thought everyone came from big families.

Catholic School Sex Ed

Yes, I grew up in a family of 16 children, born in the fall of 1967, the fifth child in this constellation, only two minutes before my twin sister popped out. We were part of a dying breed—big Catholic farm families. Same mother, same father. We kids were the offspring of "Vatican Roulette." Birth control was forbidden in Catholic households. We were all born over a 17-year period—or was it no periods?! On top of that I have 91 first cousins, just to throw that in for good measure in case anyone is counting. Good luck with that.

Early on, I couldn't figure out why the nuns at school didn't have babies. My mother told me it was because they weren't married. So then, I wanted to be a nun too. That explanation satisfied me for a while, until sixth grade, when we had a class planned for us big girls to learn about menstruation. I didn't know what that big word meant, but it sounded impressive, and I was proud to be able to flaunt it. The school sent a note home, and I started telling everyone I saw about the upcoming special class, including telling people on my paper route. I shared this in a sing-songy way: "I get to go to a class about menstruation. La la la la la lahhhh."

There was a class on the same day for the big boys, about "ejaculation." Another big, impressive word.

Then we would all get together as a group and ask whatever questions we had. This was a special time for us big kids. I thought the meeting had something to do with graduating from 6th grade, celebrating a passage, and planning a party.

After the class, I was so embarrassed! How would I face all the people I had tried to impress?

A boy in the combined class had drawn stick figures of a naked couple having intercourse and passed it around. We were told only married people could have intercourse. When I saw the picture I thought, "Yuck, gross, no way, my parents would never do that." Another boy looked at the drawing and immediately ripped it up. He told the teacher someone was drawing bad pictures. Welcome to sex ed. Those two hours changed the world I had known. I couldn't look at my parents the same way again without imagining what they had secretly been up to. It would take me a while to accept the fact that they sometimes got naked together, at least 15 times. I don't remember learning that impregnation rarely happens the first go around—that a woman is only fertile a few days out of each month. How did my parents keep this on the down low in a house that was bursting from the seams with offspring? Never mind! Now I thought I better never get married!

My Parents

Besides producing a large family, my dad was a skilled bricklayer, and an awesome gardener. He built houses, schools, clinics, and gas stations. When our family grew out of the first house he built for us, he designed a bigger one and recruited his buddies to help construct it. The new one had six bedrooms and two bathrooms to accommodate ten of us in tow, which became eighteen of us. The exterior of the new house was made of beautiful golden limestone bricks. Our dad told us the house was built for a tornado. A smaller family, friends of my parents with four kids, bought our old house and commented later that they needed two additions for their family of six. Our last name could've been changed to Sardines. It's all *relatives*, if you get my drift.

Every morning before my dad went off to work, he kissed my mother goodbye. Every night when he got home, he kissed her again. I never saw them fight. I'm grateful for that sweet and genuine display of affection.

My parents had met at a diner where my mom was working as a waitress when she was a senior in high school. Dad was passing through town on a job, catching his meals at the diner. They were attracted to each other and started to date almost immediately. He was quite a bit older than my mom and had been a sailor in the Navy. My mom looked up to him, so proud of this handsome man who had served his country. He gave her heart and her body the flutters big time.

At that time my dad was building "filling" (gas) stations, traveling from town to town, even working in other states. He'd visit my mom on weekends, always staying alone at a local motel. She didn't visit him there; it wasn't allowed. They could instead hang out at the diner. My dad was a respectable man, dropping his date off at home by 10 PM, curfew time, where her parents were waiting up. While on the road, he wrote her romantic love letters. She liked being called "hon," and "darling." My mom waited painstakingly for the love letters to come—it was the days of snail mail. Imagine the anticipation. In the short time of knowing each other my dad proposed. But my mom had half a year of high school left and made him wait until she graduated.

My dad had some heavy stories that he rarely talked about from his two tours of active duty during World War II. On the first tour, his ship was hit by Kamikazes. He worked in the hangar of the ship where the planes were housed. On a day when most of the planes were out, their landing area was targeted and struck. A man standing next to Dad on the ship pulled him down to protect him from the impact just as a Kamikaze plane was about to hit the deck, and it saved his life. He told us that as he struggled to get up everything was so horribly surreal: plane wreckage with living and dead bodies strewn here and about and a huge hole in the deck.

The sailors threw the dead bodies and wreckage into the sea while fast and furiously rebuilding the deck in record time so that their Navy planes had a place to land before running out of gas. Eerie cries for dear life could be heard from men hanging onto rafts in the cold water as the surviving sailors worked in shock. After the repairs were done, Dad looked for the hero who had saved his life. He was disappointed in never finding him.

Shortly after that bombing, he was sent home to recover from battle fatigue, which is what PTSD was called back then.

On his second active tour, he told me whenever he heard planes overhead, he was so nervous that when he sat down his legs would walk in place by themselves. A week after Hiroshima was bombed, his aircraft carrier stopped at their port. He made his way through the wreckage taking pictures, none of which turned out because of the amount of radiation in that war zone.

From the horrors of war, for the rest of his life my dad lived with PTSD. Dad kept the war at bay by being a workaholic, a chain smoker, raising 16 kids, keeping a garden, and drinking on Friday nights. This unconscious strategy seemed to work for him only while we were growing up. It came to haunt him later on in life. After he retired, I don't know how he managed to go on with flashbacks and bad dreams chasing him. What I do know is that my parents were both made of steel.

The Baby of the Family

Adding to the complexity of this prolific brood of offspring, my youngest brother, Chris, the 16th baby, was born with Down Syndrome. I was 11 years old. The doctors asked my mother if she wanted them to let my brother die because he also had a bad heart condition. She was shocked and told them to do what they could to keep him alive. My parents' focus of attention then went into sorting and adapting through the challenges this brought. I remember my mom crying a lot and I didn't know why. My parents never cried. They were strong. We needed them to be strong.

When Chris was about a month old, my mom had us kids sit together for a family meeting. We were afraid she was going to tell us something scary. She told us Chris had Down Syndrome, and he would not learn things as quickly as we did. She said we could all learn some sign language because his speech would be delayed. His motor development would kick in around the time he learned to walk and signing would help us understand him. I thought, "How cool is that? What was the big deal?" Afterall, he was one of us.

Chris was the greatest gift my family received. He was and still is so full of charisma and love. He taught us compassion and understanding in living with a "different ability."

Chores

The oldest of us kids had to pitch in, often taking on child rearing responsibilities for our younger siblings between the punches of sibling rivalry. I was assigned to Chris and started learning American Sign Language (ASL) from the weekly tutor who came to work with him, along with what I could memorize from a sign language book.

In the short growing season of our northern Maine climate, my family grew a large vegetable garden, thankfully without the petrochemicals that were becoming more and more prevalent. When we kids weren't propagating plants, pulling weeds, harvesting, canning, or selling vegetables at the farmers market, we looked for four-leaf clovers and snakes, rode bikes, tied each other to trees, and followed the creek bed behind our house. We often brought home agates, tadpoles, bluebells—whatever we could find. I remember us playing different kinds of outdoor games, including hide-and-go-seek, kickball, red rover, and baseball.

The girls helped babysit, keep the house clean, prepare meals, and wash dishes. Every other day there was laundry to wash and then hang on the line all year round—our clothes were freeze-dried in the wintertime, adding a fresh outside smell. To this day I hang clothes out all year, enjoying the fresh scent.

Once I begged my dad for a dishwasher. He said he already had ten daughters taking care of that. The boys did the outside work, mowing the lawn, working in the garden and shoveling snow in the winter. We "dishwashers" thought the boys had it easy because their work ended after dinner. "It just wasn't fair," we thought. In our defense, a mean thing we would say to them was, "You were adopted because your parents didn't want you, and we don't want you either, nah nah nah nah nah."

Farm Excursions

Sometimes on a weekend, a few of us would visit a former neighbor, Hanna, on her farm. To get there the fastest way required walking over a tall, quarter mile long train trestle. We had to listen for trains before we crossed, then be cautious going over, both for navigating the height and to avoid unexpected trains. There were a few small four-foot square platforms with railings built on the sides of the trestle to escape on (that's what we thought) if we were caught by a passing train, but they didn't look or feel safe.

At the farm we learned to ride horses, bale hay, milk goats and gather eggs. One afternoon when it was threatening rain, we headed for home early from the farm planning to beat the pending downpour. With our umbrellas in hand, I asked my sister Sue if she wanted to pretend playing Mary Poppins with me. At the end of the train trestle, where there was the shortest drop with a pile of sand below, I said it looked like a soft landing. "I'll go first," I offered, and opened my umbrella, then carefully jumped off the edge. We didn't expect gravity to win. It was probably a 12-foot drop, and I landed hard, luckily without breaking anything, except maybe my tailbone. I do remember that I couldn't play jump rope or go horseback riding for a long time after that.

Winter Fun

In the wintertime, which sometimes lasted six months, we watched a lot of TV, played cards, board games, and cribbage, in between reading seed catalogs. Outside, we built snow forts, went tobogganing, licked icicles, and walked the frozen creek bed, returning home to steaming hot chocolate. I can still taste it. There was never a want for something to do as we navigated our childhood years. On the spur of the moment, we pulled magic out of our hats.

The Paper Route

A shared newspaper route divided among several of us, and passed down like our hand-me-downs, was a family monopoly. This allowed us poor church mice to earn some money. One of the families on my route had a deaf daughter, June, who I would see on weekends and in the summertime when she was home from the residential School for the Deaf. We would wave at each other and smile when I delivered the paper. Sometimes she would be home on my collection nights. I always enjoyed being able to have a rudimentary conversation with her in American Sign Language.

On "collection nights" we went door-to-door to our neighbors, collecting money for their newspaper subscriptions. When we got home, our earnings, minus what we owed the newspaper company, were divvied up and stuffed into a wide variety of colorful socks. My mother set up this mini home banking system for us to keep our savings in. There was a unique design or color for each kid and masking tape to mark our names.

As the money built up, some was deposited into a bank account. Dipping into our savings involved negotiating with our mother, who helped us discern what we needed, or not, sometimes to our disappointment. I remember buying things like cartons of milk and ice cream so I didn't have to drink the gross powdered milk my mother made, and so I could have dessert more than one night a week. Buying a private food stash didn't last long because my siblings would separately and secretly sneak my milk and ice cream, each assuming I wouldn't notice. It was hard to figure out who to blame.

I was jealous of other kids who didn't have to work so hard and got lots of nice things, especially after Christmas when we would return to school and hear about the piles of gifts they opened. Compared to other kids all I usually got from Santa was some utilitarian piece of clothing like socks or underwear and a dumb ol' cheap toy. When I found out Santa wasn't real, I was so mad about the lie and told my other younger siblings and classmates. They would deny it. I remember arguments about whether or not I was telling the truth and later kids being mad at me for spoiling a secret.

The paper route became a hand-me-down, kind of like the clothes we wore being passed on to younger siblings. That freed us up to take on other responsibilities.

Volunteer Work

Giving back to the community was an important value instilled in our family. We all found ways to offer a few hours each week for volunteer service.

My first gig was as a Candy Striper at a local hospital. We wore red and white striped smocks to identify us: life-size candy cane people who passed out sweetness. That job entailed taking direction from the nurses as to where we could be most useful in assisting with patient needs. I remember lovely heartfelt patient interactions.

My next volunteer position was at a state mental asylum (institutions that began to close in the 1980's; none were remaining by 2015). I spent time walking the halls with patients getting them out of their rooms. One of the patients, a thin bent over frail man, seemed to enjoy meeting imaginary people who would appear out of nowhere through cracks in the floor. He would laugh uproariously and then look at me with a sheepish toothless grin. I thought this guy was loco, along with other wackadoodle patients, until I had an experience with LSD.

That altered state gave me much insight! I could see how patients' chemistry sets might have them tripping all the time—no stop button. Luckily, I didn't have an addictive personality and from a onetime hit, I gained a realistic interpretation of an aspect of the world of psychedelics. By age 15 I had dabbled in pot smoking and small amounts of alcohol consumption, but those were tame comparatively. From my acid trip, an enjoyable hallucinogenic out of body experience, I developed empathy, compassion, and a new perspective about the patients I worked with.

Lost in the Shuffle

Growing up in a big brood didn't leave room for being bored. We juggled carefree playtime with lots of responsibility. There wasn't time to address complaints. Competing for our parents' individual attention was a drive that mostly went unnoticed or unsatisfied.

On days when I could break away from the intensity of so many people living under one roof, I would walk to the local park where the train went by, waiting to hear the sound of passing railcars and the whistle, up close. We could hear it in the distance from the doorstep of our house.

With so much going on all around me, I learned to be resourceful, while being conditioned to work. Amidst all the busyness I did feel deprived of parental attention. I threatened to run away several times, in part to get away from my older brothers.

I only managed to run away once when I was five, which scared me. I brought myself home after it got dark, without anyone noticing I had been gone for six hours. I needed to go to the bathroom. Number two. The outdoor playhouse down the street where I was hiding didn't have one, and I had learned that it wasn't proper to pee or poop outside. I pooped in my pants and when the stench got to me I went back home, sneaking in, then sat in my soiled pants until my mother noticed the smell. I can still hear her say, "Oh, Samantha why did you poop in your pants?!" She cleaned me up without any more questions—no biggie for her in the "diaper factory."

At 15, while I was planning to run away, I was offered a nanny job by friends I babysat for who were moving 40 miles away. They offered me free room and board, a small allowance, and drove me to a part time waitress job. It was a win-win escape! I still babysat, cooked meals, did the laundry, and cleaned, without batting an eye. *Sound familiar?* For the first time I had my own bedroom and only two kids to take care of!

This gave me a needed reprieve from shadow parts of family life, especially with a mean big brother, and channeled my energy into familiar responsibility. At the end of the summer my mother wouldn't let me stay on for the next school year. She was afraid she would lose me for good, saying she wanted to enjoy the last few years of me living at home.

Abuse

I had to deal with my scary oldest brother again. He acted like he was a king with power to order us around. If we didn't follow his demands we would get beat up when my parents were gone, while he and my oldest sister were in charge. My parents occasionally would spend a weekend away visiting some of my dad's family who lived three hours away.

I was one of the few who resisted my bully of a brother, but then there was hell to pay. Getting beat up went from name calling and other verbal taunting to being pounded (hit hard with his fist), which sometimes escalated to being pinned down on the floor to be pounded on the upper chest 99 times (called the "terrible 99"). While I wailed, it sent chills down the spine of onlooking siblings who then didn't dare set themselves up for such treatment. My parents didn't believe my complaints about him—he didn't leave a mark.

There were other things I wanted my parents to know also—secrets about that brother I thought I couldn't or shouldn't divulge. His sexual advances started out with me getting tied to a bunk bed post, with only one escape. He hid candy in his pockets and under his clothes in various places on his body. I had to find all the candy using one forehand and hand free from the bindings while not untying myself; I had to first pull candy out of his pockets and feel around his body on the outside of his clothes until I found it all. The candy was an incentive, and I went along with the game, not thinking much of it.

An advantage with my brother that I didn't want to lose was that "if I behaved," he was a pipeline for access to alcohol, pot, and speed; things I didn't have time to involve myself with much but used on occasion as an escape from life's stressors. When he offered me heroin and started asking for sexual favors and making further sexual advances in exchange, I realized this was going too far.

The abuse stopped when I FINALLY threatened to tell my parents on him (but just hadn't sooner, out of fear of repercussions). Sadly, then other siblings had to bear the abuse, which I only found out about much later.

My hero during the times when I needed to be strong was Popeye.

High School Employment

By age 16 we all were hired for various jobs, besides going to school, volunteering, and working our butts off at home. I started out with a part time cleaning/mothers helper job for a family of ten kids. I did that only for a few months, until the oldest son pulled me into his bedroom one day and forced kisses on me.

After that I got a job as a maid in a hotel, then as a cashier at a grocery store, later being promoted to bookkeeper. Several of my siblings were hired at the same store in various departments. We were all worker bees with a good reputation. The jobs were fun, and with all the friends we made at work, it was a nice enough social life to keep us out of trouble. Who had time for that?

My First Romance

And at age "sweet 16 and never been kissed," while sitting on the train tracks one day, grabbing some solace like I would often do, June found me and introduced me to her friend, Dave. He was a cute kid with thick brown hair, wearing a plaid cotton shirt and well-worn Levi's over his hairy body. He was my age. June was secretly matchmaking.

Dave had Deaf parents and I found it intriguing to learn that sign language was his first language. His parents communicated in American Sign Language, so he was fluent. We all sat together signing, me making all kinds of mistakes, but Dave was patient and we were soon laughing together. He was funny and fun to be with. In a short time, he became my first sweetheart.

Dave stood six foot two, and his eyes changed color from blue to green depending on the light. He was like a big teddy bear, towering over my five-foot four height and skinny frame. He got to know my family pretty well over time, especially my brother, Chris; he could understand his rudimentary signing and sign back to him. I learned new signs from both of them while learning from June. Dave, with his strong build, helped us a lot in the garden. He taught me signs for carrot, onion, strawberry, rake, and, when he taught me the sign for "make love," I blushed and walked away. We all grew so fond of him. My parents secretly wished he and I would end up together. So did his parents. What would he say if I told him I never wanted kids?

When I didn't have the train tracks to sit by, on rainy days or during the cold winter months, I would curl up with a blanket on a dirt floor in what we called the "fruit room," a root cellar where we stored our canning goods, heirloom seeds, and other garden bounty. I would have my book of quotes to read—literary gems I had been collecting since second grade. I copied these quotes from bulletin boards, off teachers' doors at school, from the greeting card section of the local five-and-dime, wherever I could find them. If I was having a bad day, I could open up my collection and read the inspiring words. They would lift me up out of any funky mood. Dave and I started reading the quotes we collected to each other.

And Dave taught me more sophisticated signs, like how to swear and the names for the 50 states, as well as countries around the world. He knew I was interested in traveling. We would half sign, half talk our conversations. One Saturday morning we took off our shoes and ran in the wet dewy grass. I slipped and he caught me. With his face so close, I could smell cinnamon gum on his breath. He signed "gum," then pretended to chew my fingers, then my hand, and moving his mouth up to mine, started kissing me passionately. I didn't resist! When we reluctantly broke from our spontaneous kissing, he was blushing, and I was too. We knew we didn't have a lot of extra time to be together like this, so we reveled in the moment.

Theatre

One of my best high school memories and a great confidence builder was getting the lead role in the comedy, *Arsenic and Old Lace*. My friend Roberta convinced me to audition to be one of the dead bodies in the play-I would still be able to go to work and wouldn't need to be at all the rehearsals with a bit part. It sounded like a fun idea, and I had wanted to volunteer backstage as I could. That way, between my job and helping out in the theater, there'd be no time to get stuck babysitting at home.

For the audition the director had everyone at tryouts read the same script. I didn't have stage fright until I got assigned to the lead role: one of the two spinster sisters who felt sorry for crotchety old men. They served them wine tainted with arsenic and buried their dead bodies in the cellar. Since I had already determined I never wanted to have kids, I wondered if the spinster sister role was my fate.

I had a setback after the play; I got sick with mono that landed me in bed for about a month. I was teased about having the "kissing disease." Dave was the only one I was kissing those days, and he didn't have it. I found out it can be transferred from drinking glasses or sharing silverware. I guess I needed something to slow me down from the buzz of activity that was my life. My immune system had worked on overload with lack of sleep and skipped meals.

At the end of the school year, I received a trophy for "Featured Actress" and was invited into the Thespian Club, a great honor for a fledgling actress.

Being the Butt End of Jokes

Throughout my school years there were plenty of taunts connected to my gargantuan sized family. It wasn't fun but perhaps it built strength for dodging insults and helped me learn how to think for myself. In a history class we once were asked: "Who was the father of mass production?"

Someone shouted, "Mr. Song, Samantha's father."

One time, on a debate team, I had picked the topic of Zero Population Growth to defend. I gave good arguments and could have won the debate. What I think lost it for me was a smart aleck in the back of the room who knew I was from an unusually large family. He called out in a sarcastic tone, "Tell them the truth, tell them how many brothers and sisters *you* have." I was caught off guard and didn't want to admit that my own parents had contributed a pack of kids to populating the planet. Without a quick retort, I feebly answered that it had nothing to do with the topic, but it had taken the wind out of my sails.

When I got home, I did some math and had a brilliant answer to illustrate exponential growth. If I had thought of that in advance, I could've used it to show how long it would take to stabilize the population. At least I convinced myself that to make up for my parents' proliferation, my siblings and I had to have *negative* 14 children and join the die-off of those not reproducing on the planet.

The Travel Bug

By age 18 I had become an independent young woman with the attitude that I could do anything I set my mind to. I had sworn off being tied down with raising kids in my adult life.

I wanted to be free to travel the world. With college grants, scholarships, and my $8,000 savings I was set for a while, and I deserved a break. I took a leave of absence from my job. My boss told me he'd offer me a part-time position when I got back.

I boxed up a few of my sentimental possessions and stored them in the "fruit room," where I would retrieve them after a trip around Europe for two months. Within hours of packing my suitcase, my room had been taken over, looking like I had never lived there. I was moving to a college dorm after I returned so I guessed that was okay, but I felt a little sad that there was no sign that I had even existed there.

I was about to embark into the unknown. I could taste my freedom!

Dave saw me off. He had listened to my stance about not having kids, but he thought I would change my mind. I argued that there were plenty of families wanting children, and the world was already over-populated. "Procreation of so many families in the US who live high off the hog seems like the single most destructive act anyone could do to our Mother Earth," I said.

"You'll change your mind," he replied.

"Dave, I have pretty much already raised kids. It's too much work. As far as my siblings are concerned, I wish someone would adopt them all!

11
Freedom

WHAT DOES FREEDOM LOOK LIKE? In this instance I was free of sibling duties, rivalries, chores, and parental authority. It was so exciting stepping out into a whole new world! Travel and college were at my doorstep.

My mom had wanted one of her ten daughters to become a nurse. To thank her for giving me life and to please her, I picked a local college with a 2-year RN program. Medical settings were not foreign to me. Volunteer jobs in my teens gave me some semblance of familiarity with the territory.

Shortly after returning from my vacation traveling solo through Europe (that's a different story full of adventure) on a rainy day in August, I moved my boxes and a few meager possessions out of my family's house to a furnished dorm for female nursing students. My room was at the end of a long dark corridor. We had skeleton room keys that made lots of noise when they were turned to unlock the deadbolts locks—metal against metal. Inside the room was an outdated wallpaper print with a gross, giant flower pattern in dull shades of gray and green. "Blech!" I thought, but at the same time I was grateful, and I knew I could find some posters to cover some of the gaudiness.

Students tucked themselves away to study in their own rooms. When their large, heavy, solid wood doors opened with a creaking noise and then closed, the loud banging created a disturbing hollowness that echoed down the otherwise deathly quiet hallway. The shared bathrooms and showers were only a few doors down from my room. These things weren't noise to me; it was comforting to have the familiarity of live people around. Outside of toilet flushes, water running, people walking in the halls, doors banging, the general tone of the place was an eerie stillness.

I had excitedly anticipated getting away from the constant commotion and responsibilities of home, and it was a great privilege to have my own bedroom with a desk! However, it didn't take long for this exciting newness to wear off. Living on my own became the loneliest feeling I had ever had.

My best friend June had recently moved to Washington, DC to attend Gallaudet University, whose main student body was about 1500 Deaf students. I was excited for June and looked forward to visiting her. I missed her and my family terribly. I would call home often just to hear familiar voices. I even enjoyed the background murmur of their dinner cacophony.

I hadn't expected to be homesick living in the dorm. Even though my family was only ten miles away, between my part-time bookkeeping job, my full college load, and with no easy means of transportation, they could just as well have been living on the moon.

Almost from the day I started nursing school, I had been encouraging my twin sister, Noreen to join me in the program. She hadn't chosen a major yet. We discussed the possibility of studying together and supporting one another through a challenging program. Best of all, as nurses, we would be able to find jobs easily. We could travel the world. That dream excited *me,* at least. I was the one with wanderlust. To my delight, Noreen decided to join the nursing program, and we found an affordable apartment to share. She too had been ready to move out of our family's home, and I gladly left that lonely dorm behind. Fortunately, we seemed to have outgrown some of the competitive nature of being twins, at least outwardly.

We enjoyed the opportunity to share in a quiet household and study together.

In a psychology class that second semester, I met both a Deaf student and the American Sign Language (ASL) interpreter who interpreted the class. Since I knew some conversational sign language, we quickly became friends. On the rare occasions when June came home, it was also fun to have another signing friend to hang out with. These friendships planted the seed for contemplating working with the Deaf community; maybe I could interpret in medical settings.

Nursing Assistant Job

When school let out that first year, I took a new job in my field of study as a nurse's aide in a nursing home. That was a bittersweet experience for me, as I would fall in love with my patients and some of them would die. Holding a dying patient's hand as they took their last breath was a profound experience. Giving them a final bath, waiting for the morgue to pick up the corpse—all of it was pretty intense. I often felt so sad.

Seeing my patients waste away, weakening daily as their health failed did more than make me sad, however. It piqued my own interest in learning about my diet and in getting more exercise. Wasn't there a better way to age so as not to come to the end of one's life lingering for years in a nursing home?

When it came to death and dying, my questions led me to learning about the Hospice movement, with its focus on quality, not quantity of life. I found this so intriguing and hoped this movement would lead to the standard protocol for all. My day would come too, and it was never too soon to write a will, assign a power of attorney, a medical power of attorney, and complete the "Five Wishes" to get my ducks in a row before I would be too sick to make choices and be at the mercy of an unsustainable system.

On my job I got to witness all the charting and administrative oversight the nurses had to do. That would mean less direct contact with patients, the part I enjoyed most. And I was starting to really question Western medicine, which seemed so constricted by its heavy emphasis on the pharmaceutical approach to illness and excessive medical interventions with hardly any attention given to ways of promoting and maintaining health and wellness. There was very little focus on good nutrition, exercise, and lifestyle coaching. Why? I realized there was no money in that. I felt, and still feel strongly today, that Western medicine's focus needs to be more about "health" care, not "wealth" care or "sick" care.

I started putting time and energy into pursuing preventative medicine practices. The first book I picked up was *Sugar Blues*. I experimented with their healthy eating regimen, and soon discovered I was feeling better simply by avoiding the hidden sugars in processed food and adding a little more activity in my life. Why wasn't that taught in nursing school?

Changing College Majors

Before starting my second year of college, I decided to follow my heart and quit nursing school. This was partly because Noreen seemed to be enjoying her studies so much. I hoped she would satisfy our mother's wish to have at least one nurse in the family.

Since I was still interested in healthy lifestyle practices, I decided to pursue majoring in health and wellness. I figured that, if things didn't work out, I could always go back to finish nursing school. I kept my job as a nurse's aide, something I enjoyed, but I also kept trying to find my niche.

I began branching out, taking courses in complementary medicine, social studies, philosophy, and world religions as well as fun electives including studying piano and calligraphy. I finished all the general education requirements (English, Math, and Spanish) to get an Associate of Arts (AA) degree. Meanwhile, the perfect college emerged as I searched for other options to further my education: Empire State College, in Rochester, New York. I was interested in everything, sometimes finding it hard to narrow down and focus my studies. At Empire State, I could design my own curriculum and get credit for the wide array of learning pathways I was on.

Not the Marrying Kind

Dave and I had continued interweaving our lives around maintaining a relationship during my first few years in college. When I knew I'd be moving away soon with new pursuits, I felt it was a good time to say our goodbyes.

On our last walk down to the train tracks, Dave was excited about showing me something. He crouched down on his hands and knees, put his ear to the ground, listening for a train, and then pretended he had just discovered a fascinating object.

"Look, Samantha. I found a treasure!" he said and then held up a small diamond ring. "Will you," he gulped, and then started over. "Will you marry me?"

I was dumbfounded. I did not know what to say. I almost couldn't breathe.

"Say something," said Dave.

"I can't. I'm still in shock. This is just so unexpected, Dave, and so sweet!" I didn't know how to tell him I didn't want a ring. "I—

ah—I thought we decided we wanted different things and it wouldn't work to get hitched. Didn't we agree we were going to be just friends?"

"I want to marry you, Samantha. Won't you marry me?"

"No, Dave, honey, friend, buddy—uhhhhh—I can't. You want to have kids, and you'll never talk me into that. I want my freedom. You wouldn't be happy," I cried.

"You have no idea what you are talking about," he replied. "Okay, you don't want kids now, but how do you know you never will? I can wait. We don't have to rush it. Please?"

He pleaded with me. Then he argued with me. Before long, we were both crying, wiping tears away on our sleeves. I was too afraid to give him any comfort in this tender moment; I was afraid I'd wind up saying *Yes* and regretting it for the rest of my life.

"No," I said. "No, I can't. How can I show you that I still love you, but I'm just not the marrying kind of girlfriend?"

"Oh, Samantha," Dave said, "trying to hold on to you is like trying to catch a greased pig."

I laughed, and then he did too. He held the ring up to the sunlight and it caught a beautiful beam of light. Then he offered it to me again, signing the "I love you" sign.

I pushed his hand away, and then I signed to him, "I told you, I can't." Then I started walking back to my car, tears flooding my eyes. Dave walked beside me in silence. When we reached my car, we hugged each other tightly and said our goodbyes. Later, I discovered he had surreptitiously slipped the ring inside my purse.

"Thank you, Dave. I'm sorry. Please forgive me. I love you."

I went home thinking I'd feel better if I leafed through my book of quotations to find some words of comfort. Instead, I grabbed *Green Eggs and Ham* by Dr. Seuss, my favorite childhood book.

As the plot unfolds, Sam-I-Am is trying to convince the little boy in the story to try green eggs and ham, but the boy refuses. In funny rhymes. I thought of how Dave had tried to convince me to marry him. To me, that meant he wanted me to settle down, have a family, and give up the exciting, full life I'd always dreamed of.

Inside my head, I began to answer him in short rhymes like those used by Dr. Seuss:

"No, I will not marry you
Not in a boat or with a goat;
Not in the rain or on a train;
Not in a box, Nor with a fox;
Not in a tree—I want to be free!"

Over the next several days I wrote a fun story as a way to process my sadness. It was called: "Save the Gorillas," based on the times Dave would dress up for parades we were in. It included a reference to being afraid of gorillas and running away.

When I finished the story, I called Dave to express some of my reluctance and sadness about the finality of our breakup. I was in pain, and I didn't want to regret my decision. He thought that I might change my mind and say "yes." All that phone call did was cause confusion and more frustration on his part.

As much as my heart ached, I was determined not to interrupt my life's various callings with a relationship destined to tie me down to a person or a place, and certainly not with a whole pack of rugrats. I didn't want to lose my freedom.

I called him when I discovered the ring, asking about dropping it off to him, but Dave wouldn't take it back. I tucked it away in a small jewelry box that I rarely used. Makeup, jewelry, nice clothes

—these weren't necessary for me. I needed them only for job interviews and, yes, sometimes for other people's weddings. I was free!

12
Learning Curves

I MOVED AWAY TO ATTEND Empire State College. At this school, students work with an advisor in developing learning contracts. They then meet with mentors who help them document the flow and completion of each contract. Online classes are often woven into the plan. I created a Bachelor of Science degree in Interdisciplinary Studies, still focusing my studies in the areas of health and wellness.

Renting a room from two single sisters who were college educated and now retired proved to be school in itself. They modeled for me independent adventurous lives engaged in community and travel, and so resourceful. Considered "old maids" perhaps by those who were jealous of their lifestyles, but I was intrigued by them. They were so supportive and kept me updated on local happenings and the news. I am forever grateful for their guidance.

I was able to land a job as a nursing assistant at a hospital near the college. My job was working as a "float"—a nursing assistant who works on whichever floor was short staffed that day. Through that job, I stayed connected to the medical field and kept learning through exposure and experience in every department in the hospital.

My school curriculum included getting credit for taking online courses in microbiology, anatomy, and chemistry, combined with hands-on learning. One memorable hands-on course was an Emergency Medical Training class. Because the course covered how to treat a heart attack, we were given the opportunity to watch open heart surgery. Another time, I had the opportunity to witness a live birth. I saw the pain of childbirth in the twisted face of the mother. I remembered her screams, her exhausted moans, the sweat that poured down her face and matted her hair. I could not fathom why anyone would be willing to go through that.

Afterwards, I called my mother to ask how she had survived giving birth sixteen times?! Rather nonchalantly, my mother said that she never remembered the pain. She said when my sister Elizabeth, her twelfth birth, was born breech, she'd hardly even felt it at all. From what I'd witnessed I would never choose to bear a child. Never.

Adding Deaf Studies to My Curriculum

June came to visit for a weekend when I was trying to figure out how to *marry* my interests in healthy living and working with the Deaf community. She told me that Gallaudet had a program for "special students," and encouraged me to apply. I learned from her that up to fifteen hearing undergraduates were accepted each year and could attend the college for the maximum of one year. Credits would get transferred back to the home college. I figured I might get accepted if I added Deaf Studies to make a double major. At the time I couldn't find any Deaf Studies programs in the US and where else to go but a mecca for Deaf people? Pulling off a double major would mean adding an extra year of school. Did I want to do that?

I decided I did. In fact, I jumped at the opportunity, applying the same week. To my delight, within a month, I was accepted as a cross-registered student. I looked forward to being study buddies with June! We would both spend our senior year in college together.

In order to complete one more learning contract during the summer before my move to Washington, DC, I attended the Hippocrates Institute's *Life Transformation Program* in West Palm

Beach, Florida. The program included a great detoxification and immune system booster. It was yet another class packed with information and strategies to add to my toolbox of both self-care and teaching goals.

At Gallaudet, I was challenged to find myself as a minority student. Not having been born into Deaf culture, I felt overwhelmed and isolated. I was an outsider. Students had "well-meaning" hearing people making decisions for them all their lives. At Gallaudet they felt empowered and supported to be themselves. I represented a whole culture of people they experienced as being discriminated by. I couldn't even sign in their language fluently. Was there anything I could do to feel as though I belonged there, even a little bit? Luckily, I had June as an ally.

I worked hard on improving my command of ASL. Fluency in any language comes through sustained daily practice. There was a language lab I could study in with and an ample supply of videotapes that demonstrated and gave me more exposure to ASL. And I had plenty of interaction with the language in my classes. Deaf students newer to learning ASL were more patient with my *accent*—they had one too. Some had been prohibited from using sign language in school programs where they grew up, and many of them lived in families who never learned their language.

I also had a part-time job interpreting phone calls between Deaf and hearing people at a call center on campus; not all students had teletype phones at that time, and it was before video relay services were available.

With June's support, I found two professors who were sensitive to my plight as a minority student. I was one of fifteen hearing students in a Deaf society. They took me under their wings. From them, I learned about oppression, discrimination, and reverse discrimination—when discrimination gets projected back on to the targeted oppressor. They taught me to imagine myself as a student in a foreign country. Doing so helped me understand the kinds of challenges Deaf people face every day, living in a mostly hearing world.

These new understandings saved me from taking personally the taunts I endured as a hearing student in a Deaf world. Nevertheless, with time and patience, I began to earn the trust of Deaf students and developed a network of friends from around the country. We vowed to stay in touch, and indeed our lives were to crisscross over the next many years. They still do, to this day.

Back in Rochester, NY, I finished out my double major in part by attending a semester-long Interpreter Training Program. My final college semester was spent writing learning contracts with Deaf professors from the National Technical Institute for the Deaf (NTID), one of the ten colleges at the Rochester Institute of Technology. The added major gave me versatility for future possibilities working with both the Deaf and hearing communities.

After five years of college, I had set my ideals on living, modeling, and teaching a healthy lifestyle that I hoped others might follow. Unlike many young college women, I was definitely not going there for my "Mrs." Degree.

Graduate School

As my life unfolded, I kept discovering so much more that I wanted to learn about, including the health of the planet and how it impacts us physically. I was ripe for learning and was happy to find Gaia University, which had a satellite training center in the US. Their foundations coursework and curriculums designed by students included credits for experiential hands-on learning. A whole new world and network opened up to me! I chose to continue my studies through them pursuing a Master's degree in Natural Health and Applied Ecology.

The program began the summer I graduated from Empire State. There was no time for a break, no time to waste. I started with two solid weeks taking a required foundations course called *Permaculture Design*, which was offered at an Ecovillage Training Center in Tennessee. The class was housed at "The Farm," a large intentional community of people dedicated to living in a way that had minimal impact on the environment. Permaculture was the most comprehensive system I had ever seen based on long-term sustainability of the planet. I saw it demonstrated right there where I could watch and participate daily.

The Farm also had a well-known school for midwifery. The midwives living on that land could deliver your baby, which was definitely not something I wanted to consider.

After the foundations course, I moved back home to create the rest of my curriculum, furthering my studies at Gaia. In my first semester, I took online courses in earth science and ecology.

When that first semester ended, I traveled to Belize for a semester-long internship in a Mayan village where a permaculture project had been started. I was excited to be going to a place where the people were ninety percent self-sufficient and where I could both work on that project and work directly with deaf natives.

I had previously discovered that there was a need for people to work with the marginalized deaf population in Belize. I had built a network of people eager to support a new project of my own making, serving underprivileged deaf students in classrooms. I wanted to expand that to be an official non-profit organization. Teaching sign language to families who had deaf children and perhaps to the wider native community, as well as gardening with the permaculture project, seemed like a match made in heaven.

Internship in Belize

Between flights at the Miami airport, I met another intern named Chaz. Chaz was friendly and playful, wearing denim overalls, a baseball cap and tennis shoes. I thought he was cute.

"Where are you headed?" he asked.

"Belize City, and then making my way to a Mayan village outside of Punta Gorda."

"Hey, small world! Same as me! Let's get a seat together and compare notes if you want?"

Chaz was traveling from a college in Virginia to Cancun, Mexico, the same city I was flying into. He had been studying permaculture, too. In Belize, he'd be working on the practical application of its principles. I was ecstatic to find out that his project, which was to further earlier work at a permaculture demonstration site, was in the *same* village where I was going. Chaz would be overseeing the garden crew!

Chaz was a free spirit, full of ideals and lots of energy. On the plane we learned of each other's passions for life and discovered more mutual academic interests.

When I shared with Chaz that my focus would be working with deaf students, he stopped talking and finger-spelled the entire Sign Language alphabet. (That often happened when I told a new acquaintance that I worked with deaf people. They would stop talking and slowly and hesitantly fingerspell A-B-C-D-E all the way through the alphabet, asking me to correct their errors. I always waited patiently for them to finish. Sometimes they'd even ask me if I knew Braille. I appreciated their attempts to connect with me, and always explained that Deaf people communicate through sign language, while blind people read using Braille.)

I explained to Chaz the plight of deaf students in many developing countries. Too often, they sat isolated among the hearing students, unable to hear what was being said. Because teachers didn't know how to work with them, some were put in classes with developmentally delayed students, even though they were just as intelligent as their hearing counterparts. It was a good sign when Chaz showed understanding and compassion.

It made me like him even more. We certainly realized a strong instant attraction to one another. As the plane landed, he laced his fingers into mine, and I didn't want to let go.

Hitching a Ride

"Wanna hitchhike with me to the village?" I asked. "I heard it's easy to do in Central America. I was going to take the bus, but the next one won't be here for another four hours. People are accustomed to sharing rides."

"Sure." He grinned at the offer.

"Great." With notebook paper from my journal and a marker, I scribbled out a sign with the name of the next big town, about 150 miles away. "I read Sissy Hankshaw's hitchhiking advice in *Even Cowgirls Get the Blues*, and it says to have a sign," I told him.

In no time, we were on our way. We got our first ride traveling with a Spanish-speaking family, our backpacks tied down to the top of their old station wagon. We would be working in an English-speaking country, but in border towns like the one we were in, people spoke Spanish.

Fortunately, Chaz spoke Spanish and interpreted for me. The radio was blaring songs in English, the first song a Bob Marley tune,

No Woman, No Cry. I was high on life, smiling from ear to ear as we bounced up and down on those pot-holed roads.

We passed little villages with small, simple, closely set homes with thatched roofs. It took us several rides and all day to get to Belize City. We'd have to spend the night and catch two different buses the next day to get to the village.

A Budding Romance

Nervously, we negotiated splitting the cost of a cheap motel.

Chaz solemnly agreed to stay on his own side of the bed. We hung out there for the night, getting to taste a little bit of the culture: some of the local food and, par for the course—a glass of tequila from a bottle with a worm in it. When we turned in for the night, I was relieved that Chaz respected my boundaries in bed.

The next day, we caught a first-class bus to Punta Gorda, and then a jam-packed bus to the village. We sat squished tightly together with our heavy backpacks on our laps. It didn't matter that it was uncomfortable. I was catching Chaz's natural scent. It was clean and inviting, like cold fresh lemons on a hot day. I was happy to have someone to share this new adventure with; it felt lucky to me. Our conversation never even paused; our words often overlapped as we kept pointing out yet another thing we found unusual in this new, colorful rustic surrounding.

The bus tires kicked up sand from the washboard roads, bringing dust inside the bus, but it was too hot to close the windows and, as you might imagine by now, we were too enamored with one another to pay much attention to it. When the bus finally pulled into our village, we were welcomed by the families who would be hosting us. To our mutual delight, we learned we'd be living a "walkable" ten minutes from each other.

Little kids stared at us through their big brown eyes. They wanted to touch our white hands. They giggled when Chaz and

I spoke, listening to our funny accents as we said our goodbyes, promising we'd see each other again once we got our bearings.

There were more giggles when we hugged each other goodnight.

It didn't take long for us to settle in and feel comfortable living a simple life in this lush rainforest jungle. I loved that a sustainable lifestyle, so connected to the land and the people, would be my home for this internship. I looked forward to more of the sweet budding romance that was emerging. How nice not having to go it alone with so much newness to experience.

Rustic Living

There was no electricity where I was living and no internet service anywhere in the village. We would have to wait for the weekend bus-trip to town if we wanted to get in touch with family, friends, and professors.

The bus we'd taken was an old, retired school bus on its second life serving the village. Bus capacity said forty-five passengers. Usually it was double that, averaging five people sharing a single seat and the aisle packed with standing passengers. No matter which day one chose, that twenty-five-mile trip meant sitting/standing on a smelly, overpacked bus with villagers carrying everything they hoped to sell/bring home from the market: all their fresh produce, their grain, and their live chickens. Any additional items were on laps, jammed under the seats, or tied on top of the bus. There wasn't an inch of wasted space.

On the rare occasions that I did take that ride, I usually chose to stand out of respect for the people whose home this was. But then I would be full of sweat when I arrived in town and dizzy when I got back.

Since I was unable stay in close touch with my local school liaison and other contacts through the internet, my only other option was to rely on snail mail. That meant giving my handwritten letters to the bus driver who would mail them for me in town. If there was any mail waiting for me, he would bring it back to our village. Communication with the outside world may have been difficult, but it was always possible. In case of family or another emergency, they could call the Punta Gorda police and the police would deliver a message to my liaison in town if it was urgent. Correspondence from the outside felt like a luxury, but I could do without emergencies that usually weren't good news anyway.

I enjoyed living a much less distracted life while working with the villagers. Unless that distraction involved building my connection with Chaz. But even though our friendship deepened, it was a little challenging trying to pursue a romantic relationship as there was almost no privacy in the village.

By the time the semester ended, I had accomplished what I'd set out to do. I'd learned so much from the locals! I planned to return someday to pick up where I left off. It was sad parting with Chaz; our time together had been fun loving, but we were clearly heading in two different directions. Even though we went our separate ways, we vowed to stay in touch.

Tragedy Back at Home

While I'd been in Belize, I hadn't been able to stay in touch with June. When I got back to the US, I learned she had gone through a traumatic experience and had moved back home.

June, now in graduate school, had been at an on-campus party where someone laced her drink with something that made her black out. She woke up in the middle of the night, naked, under a blanket that someone must have covered her with.

Several other partygoers were sprawled out sleeping on the floor in a room she recognized as a dorm suite. She could recall almost nothing about that night.

A few months later, June discovered she was pregnant. Being against abortion, she felt she had little choice but to return home to her family. Unfortunately, that also meant withdrawing from her master's program.

I desperately wanted to be of support but wasn't sure how. I was living at home only between my meandering higher education pursuits, but realized I could time things to be with June through her last month of pregnancy and hopefully with her for the labor and delivery.

Giving birth ended up being a painful experience for June. I was able to be there for the aftermath while she walked through the process of giving up her baby. Knowing she wasn't prepared to be a mother, she found placement with a loving family who agreed to allow her to have contact with the child as it grew. It looked like things were turning out okay, with June's baby going to a good family, bringing them the happiness that new life brings.

For the first three months of the baby's life, June supplied breast milk so the baby would have the best nourishment she could give him. Despite her close connection with the adoptive family, I was amazed by how quickly she seemed to bounce back. She pieced her life back together only missing a semester of school.

Fierce Independence

Since my breakup with Dave, I'd been afraid to reach out to him whenever I was back in Maine. I'd had plenty of romantic opportunities and experiences since we parted but was still vulnerable with my unending love for him.

New relationships were always fun, at least until the early courtship infatuation died down. If there was talk of getting serious, I would bow out gracefully, often keeping my friendship intact. I did find myself moving from one love affair to another because invariably in this dance, words like "marriage" and "children" would pop up. Those words were always the beginning of the end for me. Why ruin a good thing? I simply didn't want to be tied down. F-r-e-e-d-o-m was my watchword. There was more to life than making and caring for babies. That was *not* on my horizon. Never, ever! I was a woman on the go, interested in everything, and easily bored when the honeymoon was over. That attitude might sound flippant, but I did have my share of grief with breakups.

To finish my Master's program, I set out on an adventure which was to become the primary focus of the next five years of my life. Interning at a variety of eco-sustainability projects around the country would allow me to learn through hands-on experiences, workshops and self-study. That time included writing reports, doing research, and teaching. I would also have lots of opportunity to discover new places in my down time now that they would be within reach. I chose places near State Schools for the Deaf as a way to find part time work with the Deaf community. As I set out to follow my plan, I felt ready to save the world from impending destruction, one good deed at a time.

Despite missing my family and friends while I had been away in NY, Florida, DC, Tennessee, and Belize, my work in a warmer climate taught me that winters were optional. It had been a best kept secret when I grew up. Now I knew I didn't have to live out years freezing my hiney off! I had decided to leave Maine, to travel and learn, and hopefully to find a more hospitable climate to settle in along the way. Nothing and no one was stopping me.

13
Looking for Shangri-La

IN THE MIDST OF SLOWLY packing for the West Coast, the first destination on my grand adventure, I took a moment to find a quote for the road. Inspired again by Rumi, it read:

*...those who don't drink dawn like a cup of spring water
or take in sunset like supper, those who don't want to change, let them sleep...*

Before venturing forth to my future, I wanted some reassurance about what I was doing with my life, so I paid a psychic to give me her take on what lay in store. I recall only one thing she said: "I see three children in your future."

"Children? Not for me," I said as I left. I wanted my money back.

The warm spring air permeated my room, as I grabbed my heavy backpack, ready for the open road. I had said most of my goodbyes before to family, friends, and my beloved homeland. With each farewell my eyes still welled up with tears. Waves of fear and excitement filled me. June came to the train station with my parents. I promised I wouldn't forget them and would write home every week or so.

"I'm sorry to be running off again so soon. Please forgive me. Thank you for coming to see me off. I love you."

Returning to Maine had always provided an anchor for me in between my times of branching out to explore wider interests. I appreciated my sense of home there. It would always be there with open arms ready to embrace me on any return. Now I was giving myself to more mysteries that lay ahead.

Feeling at Home with Relatives

With my backpack strapped to my back, a bag of road snacks in one hand, and the other hand holding a one-way train ticket to the West Coast, I boarded and soon was on my way. I was looking forward to meeting some relatives for the first time, and then would be heading to my first job as a farmhand in Oregon. The familiar sound of the wheels moving along the tracks as I traveled further and further from home was only a mild comfort to me.

After three days and two nights on the train, I arrived in Seattle to a warm welcome from my aunt, uncle, and three of their ten children. They waved a big sign with my name on it and when we met, we fully embraced as if meeting long lost family.

My relatives lived in a small rural town tucked in the mountains of Washington, only two hours from where I would be living. This family provided a loving touchstone that helped me feel the deep connection of blood family. After a few days of getting to know each other, with a promise that I would be back to visit often, it was time for me to head to northern Oregon. To my surprise, rather than letting me take the bus as I'd planned, they drove me the whole way.

Another warm greeting awaited me in Oregon. My new hosts were the parents of three teens. Everyone in that household knew how to work the fields. I was provided with a canvas yurt to live in. It was set up next to a big garden.

I helped with vegetable production, sold fresh organic vegetables at the farmers market, and delivered bag loads of vegetables and flowers to members of their Community Supported Agriculture (CSA) project.

A CSA is an arrangement between farmers and consumers that leaves out the middleman. Members pay in advance for an entire growing season's worth of produce grown on that farm. In return, they receive weekly deliveries of the farm's just-picked bounty. In this way, members share with the farmers the risk they face, such as drought and other weather fluctuations, but they also enjoy organic produce at somewhat lower prices at the store.

There was so much to learn about plants unique to the region! Growing food crops in a dry climate with very sandy soil is so different from growing food on the east coast and in the warm, humid climate and nutrient-rich soil of Belize.

Within an hour of the farm was the State School for the Deaf. I volunteered there as a "Big Sister," making weekly visits to support my Deaf "Little Sister" in any way she needed. She was an adorable ten-year-old with pigtails and big brown eyes.

Over the next year, I spent many weekends with my relatives. They introduced me to the network of earth-skills gatherings. I attended one week-long event with them and they outfitted me with a tepee to live in, clothes to match the re-enacted time period of the 1800's, and a horse to ride. I learned a little bit about how to tan hides, sharpen tools, make clay pottery, identify edible plants, and cook over a wood fire.

Each one of my cousins had a particular niche: one was a blacksmith, another made leather clothing, the third did beautiful beadwork, while the fourth cared for the family's five horses. Together, as a family, they were the ones who made the teepees used in these events. I was inspired by the combined skills their family had.

Several of my male cousins worked at a sawmill and gave me a thorough tour that I found most fascinating! I saw how felled tree logs get processed from the thick trunk into 2x4's. Just like my parents, these relatives also maintained a large vegetable garden. Did this run in the family? Our connection was both heartfelt and rich in learning opportunities.

Footloose and Fancy Free

Leaving the job in Washington after my contract ended meant more sad goodbyes, but the spice of life was waiting for me as new enticements caught my fancy. I spent the next four years working on sustainable development projects around the country, finding each new job and terrain as fascinating as the previous one.

To get around without a car, I learned how to safely hop rides on freight trains, thumb the roadways, and transport other people's cars across the country. I found my next stops through the WWOOFers (Willing Workers on Organic Farms) network. I was able to take seasonal work and then move on as it suited me. Wherever I was, I loved meeting new plant species, learning about their personality, the kind of soil in which they grew best, and the kinds of plant-neighbors they preferred and thrived alongside. It was like meeting new people in so many ways!

From the Northwest, I headed to New Mexico, then later took jobs in the Midwest, then the Southeast, and finally headed back to Maine. All the while, I was hoping to find my own Shangri-La, that mystical and harmonious place we long to find.

By the time I was 30, I had traveled to 48 states, Canada, Belize, and taken a few more trips to Europe. Taking advantage of traveling between jobs and going on short weekend road trips in areas near where I was working, made it easy to chalk up another state. I visited intentional communities and ecovillages, getting an amazing view of assorted sustainable operations, while carving out my dream to learn to become as self-sufficient as possible. These opportunities fed my soul while teaching me basic practicalities of life.

Into this tapestry of new adventures, I was often able to weave in part time work at state schools for the Deaf, sometimes arranging to substitute for classes when teachers were out sick, or on leave—sometimes maternity leave. I was happy the latter wasn't me! I taught earth science, biology, and ecology, and did some freelance interpreting work.

Truth be told, amidst that busy time of my life there were plenty of playful romances. My hosts were always interested in matchmaking and while on the go I met so many interesting people. Serial monogamy was a thread I wove into the adventure. I also set boundaries early on: "I'm not interested in marriage and getting tied down with children," was my preface to anything that started tasting like seriousness. Looking back, I can reminisce on having had one long sweet honeymoon with no strings attached.

Home is Calling Me Back

Despite enjoying my five years of study, job opportunities, and travel, I began to feel a desire to return to my roots. I had been extremely frugal during that time, taking lots of budget travel trips, but only a few trips to visit my family and friends back home, and I missed them.

June and I had stayed in touch, writing to each other, calling occasionally, and now entertaining the idea of co-owning property in Maine. She appreciated my commitment to living close to the land, growing my own food, and learning the skills of an energy efficient lifestyle. As it happened, she and her partner (who had three kids) were looking for a small farm to buy. They had come across an opportunity to purchase 20 acres of farmland with a house ready to move into, along with a horse barn that could be renovated to add a living space for me. I was interested. I was just finishing up my latest job in Georgia, finally turning in all the coursework for my graduate degree, and I was chomping at the bit to get back to Maine.

In the course of making plans to return, I asked June to keep it a secret that I was coming so I could surprise my family. I told her I wanted to *visit* Dave, who, from her report, was still single.

There weren't any cars needing drivers to be transported, so I decided to hitchhike/ride the rails, keeping that to myself so as not to cause any undue worry for my mother. June said I could mail things to her house—my accumulations that had sentimental value, things that were breakable and things I couldn't haul on my back. I wanted the ease of a lighter load.

Hitchhiking

Standing alongside a busy highway entrance ramp with my backpack leaning beside me, breathing in a mixture of fresh air and gas fumes, my arm outstretched with my hitchhiking thumb, I was ready for another adventure. My heart felt the elation of freedom and trust. I had become accustomed to this mode of travel, always feeling a strong sense that the next ride would be as entertaining as them all. In my estimation this was the cheapest way to get high. I loved the experience of the unknown. I anticipated that I would get to my destination quicker than if I drove myself, and besides I had yet to own a car. I rarely waited longer than 5 minutes for a ride, unlike single males hitching rides, who often waited hours, or days.

My first ride was with a flirtatious guy driving a bread truck. When he dropped me off, he lunged towards me unexpectedly and gave me a sloppy wet kiss on my cheek, then muttered an explicative that made me want to run. Fifteen minutes later, while waiting for my next ride, I saw him off in the distance walking up the highway towards me. I got a little scared. I had been sexually assaulted on rides in the past and was wary. So, when a semi driver stopped to pick me up, I felt a surge of relief.

"Hi! Thanks for stopping! Wow, you stopped on a hill with your heavy load, and I think you saved my life!" I said as I explained my predicament. I always trusted and appreciated semi drivers. They are main arteries in our country's commerce, hardworking, and have big hearts.

This fella called himself "Brother Trucker from Muskogee." I immediately felt connected and safe with him. After letting me get situated in the passenger seat, he gave me his full handle: "I'm the trailer truckin', chicken pluckin', wheels spinnin', women grinnin', ace #1 truck driving superstar of CB and radar, diddley bee-boppin', pill poppin', refined petroleum products transportation engineer, double clutchin', put-put gear jammin', door slammin', tire bumpin', flanged faced, flat footed, liver lappin', north central Oklahoma, Brother Trucker in a four-wheel boogie buggy, surrounded by sweet thangs, sippin' on a cool one, reading the latest issue of Playboy, and rachet jawin' on my 40-channel fully transistorized receiver."

"Well, that's a fine 'how do you do', Brother Trucker. I'm Sister Sign Language Aficionado from El Mundo," I grinned.

"That's neat! Hey, what do you think about teaching me how to fingerspell the ABC's? I'll teach you how to drive my truck."

"What a deal! Really?" And with confidence I added, "I've driven tractors before and know a little about shifting gears."

He was tired after driving long hours (more than the allowed limit) and would be happy for some relief. He taught me how to shift through thirteen gears, and I got to experience another thrill—maneuvering that massive beast on a busy highway, sitting so high up above all the cars I felt for a minute like I owned the world. I could hardly believe it when the trucker fell asleep and kept sleeping for the next five hours while I drove!

Meanwhile, I had fun talking truckdriver jive on the CB radio with other truckers.

Every truck driver I ever met enjoyed the company of a passenger. I knew each had a specific destination, usually hundreds of miles from where they picked me up. They certainly were not out to get me. Instead, they had a genuine interest in helping me with a lift. They had a grand network of truck stops where they would meet and greet one another, fill up for gas, grab a shower, get some sleep, compare notes on the maintenance of semis, discuss other mechanical tinkering, and share lively conversations at the cafés where they grabbed their meals. A peek into their world, filled with such camaraderie, fed my soul.

On these trips, it was pure thrill enjoying the life of a vagabond. I got off Brother Trucker's semi in Pennsylvania at the end of his route north, where he would unload raw petroleum before heading back to Oklahoma with a load of a refined blend of fuel.

"Maybe see you on the flip flop, and have a good life if I don't," he called, waving out his window, saying he was hoping we would meet again.

I waved at him with the "I love you" sign—not a romantic gesture, just a symbol genuinely acknowledging my thanks for the ride and our brief touch of friendship. Filled with sweet satisfaction at the generous support I'd received from the wonderful people I'd met along the way, I kept moving forward, hopping a few trains, thumbing some more fun rides, and finally calling home from the truck stop just outside my hometown.

My mother answered, and when she heard my voice she asked, "Where are you?"

"Surprise! I'm home safe, Mom, just down the road at the truck stop."

"What? Samantha, are you okay?" she asked.

"No worries, Mom, I'm home."

"Glad to hear you are okay. I'll send your dad. He'll be so excited to hear that you're home! Can't wait to see you."

I too was glad to be safely home. When they say "one bad apple spoils the bunch," it's true, I had learned that. The annoyances and risks of hitchhiking, aside from the thrill of it, sometimes gave me second thoughts about continuing this mode of transportation. Still, I appreciated the efficiency of it and the wonderful people I met along the way.

One concern I had was for the women who worked the truck stops, selling their bodies to drivers who got lonely. They'd knock on the truck door at night when I was safely asleep in the driver's seat, while the trucker took a short nap in the cab of the truck in a small bed behind the seats. "Hey honey, do you want some company?" They'd say in their soft, sweet, flirtatious voice.

I would answer, "No thank you, not tonight." Then we wouldn't be bothered for the night.

Because I had experienced rides that felt and were unsafe, I had learned to defend myself with drivers who saw me as an opportunity to take advantage of. If our conversation went in the direction of sexual advances, I'd nip it in the bud. It might start with the driver asking me if I wanted to earn some money, implying paying for sexual favors. (When I was broke a few times I admit it was tempting.) I'd make up a quick story saying something like, "Well, I have Herpes and have pimples on my vagina. They ooze pus and itch terribly. You wouldn't want the pain." That would change the mood, and there were no more advances.

I found most people were good by nature; they enjoyed helping me, fulfilling a need we all have to be of service to others. Their hearts went out to a lone female standing on the side of the highway. From their eyes I was vulnerable and their good deed for the day was bringing me to safety. Often, I would get their address and send them a postcard of thanks to let them know I had arrived safely at my destination.

Tragedy Hits Again

Over the next few days of happy and heartfelt reunions, I also felt the deep relief of being home. I said I would never leave again, vowing to settle closer.

I signed up for a class at the Shelter Institute, setting my next goal on renovating June's horse barn, sight unseen but trusting June's description. I began imagining the design I'd use and decided to incorporate both passive and active solar energy for my heating and cooling needs. Excitement loomed; I could feel it.

June and her boyfriend set up a time to meet with the farm's owner. I looked forward to meeting them there but, on the day of the appointment, they didn't show up. The owner and I waited. And we waited. We weren't able to reach June by phone. I looked around for a while, picturing future possibilities.

I got home to a hysterical message to call June's family. Her mother was sobbing as she told me that June was in the hospital—she was in stable condition after a terrible car crash with her boyfriend and his three kids. She explained it involved a pickup truck. A branch had blocked a stop sign. They were driving fast and didn't see it (probably in a hurry to meet up with me). June's boyfriend, two of his three sons, AND a two-year-old in the pick-up truck were pronounced dead at the scene. June's boyfriend's surviving son was with his mother. He had survived the accident with only a few scratches. He and June were in deep emotional trauma.

Our world had literally and figuratively crashed. How would June ever recover? How could I help? Part of me blamed myself.

A few weeks later when June was discharged from the hospital, we walked to the train tracks every single day for the next week, waiting for the vibrations and noise of the passing trains, feeling their wind brush our faces. Wailing into that wind and the wall of their noise, we expressed our shared grief to the passing cars. What would we do to move on?

June decided to move in with her parents in order to process the hard things of life. Her deceased boyfriend's sons moved to their mom's house full time. June had a safe place to take time to grieve. Her maternal longing for the son she gave up for adoption intensified, adding to all the other losses. At least her birth son was still alive, and she did get to visit him once in a while, but that was hardly any consolation for her current loss. June vowed to be careful not to get too attached to anyone she might meet in the future.

Plan B

While June got re-situated, I needed to make a new plan. The annual Maine Common Ground Country Fair was about to start. At the fair, I knew I could tap into the resources of the Northeast and likely find a lead on a job.

I thought about calling Dave. I had just seen him at the funerals, but I ended up being afraid to approach him, thinking that in my vulnerable state I would be attracted to him all over again. I was still set on avoiding any relationships that hinted at getting tied down with someone wanting to have children.

At the fair there was a circle dance offered each morning to start the day.

These dances always perked me up some. The leader for this was an attractive man named Peter. Separate from being a good facilitator, as we befriended each other, I learned that he was the main cook at the Tracker Survival School, a place I had wanted to visit near the New Jersey Pine Barrens. He was from a family of eleven, didn't have children, and never wanted any!

What a great distraction it was to feel the rush of infatuation. One morning Peter was leading a dance called "Come Fall in Love with the Earth Again." I was smitten with him and sang, "Come fall in love with Peter" to myself.

After the fair ended, with Peter's business card in my hand, I got up the nerve to call him at his home number. The message on his answering machine said: "This is the home of Peter, Christine and Harry." I thought, "Dammit, he has a family," and hung up.

I was hanging on to a dream of settling down in a small home of my own, without really picturing myself sharing my space in the form of living in a committed relationship. I liked my freedom. Dating was enjoyable along with having a partner, as long as I approached it and was clear from the start that kisses and hugs and all the rest wasn't going to lead to settling down, marriage and procreation.

With the huge shift since arriving home, I started reimagining building a small, off-the-grid cabin, though I had no idea where I might do that. I wanted it to be in a community of like-minded people and for sure NOT in an area where people were building McMansions. I was still planning to take the building course at the Shelter Institute as next steps.

Before that course, however, I needed some guidance in processing my own grief and sorting out how to move on. I enrolled in a Landmark Encounter group training, hoping to jump-start the next chapter of my life. When the training ended, I felt it had given me some useful new tools that would help me continue healing more deeply. I then felt more ready to take the building course.

What I learned at the three-week intensive at the Shelter Institute gave me more confidence to move on to new pursuits, following my heart to lead me to the next unfolding opportunity.

Following the classroom learning, I got some hands-on experience with owner builders. A fellow classmate who also shared the dream of building a sustainable house joined me. We apprenticed on a variety of building projects, enjoying working together, and testing out dating. When winter hit, I chose not to pursue yet another relationship that might land me in marriage, children, and home ownership.

My Maine honeymoon had been heart-filling, heart-breaking, and short lived. I couldn't remember winter being so cold. I took the harshness personally, like a slap in the face.

With June still deep in grief and unable to move forward, I decided to set my sights on living in a more southern climate, but not so far away this time. I decided to move no further south than one day's drive from home. Maybe I could get resettled and even recruit June to move closer to me.

14
Sustainable Living, Here and Abroad

I DECIDED TO LOOK UP my old friend Chaz, and I quickly found him. He was living at the foothills of Virginia's Shenandoah Mountains, a full member of an ecovillage tucked away in a *holler*, about a 40-minute drive to town. He and a handful of other community founders shared the land.

On our subsequent long, lively, and informative phone conversation, Chaz gave me the big picture of what was developing. With his ecovillage's recent completion of a 4,000 square foot community building nestled in a wooded 325-acre plot of land, they had ample room to hold classes and events. Though this was just their first winter season of being open, they were nevertheless ready to host a community education series they called "Cabin Fever." The program, scheduled to start in a few weeks, was aimed at teaching a broad array of homesteading and community living skills. Each day of the week there would be classes on topics from gardening and herbalism to crafts and music-making, to mediation and family constellations. Phyllis, a founding community member, was scheduled to teach consensus, Enneagram, Qigong, and Meditation.

Community members had their own ongoing study groups learning Non-Violent Communication (NVC) and reading *A Pattern Language*. The study groups were focused on weaving the social fabric of people living in close proximity and sharing resources with one another. Learning how to get along with one another was felt to be just as important as the more practical courses in building houses and growing food.

The group had also scheduled local dance parties, as well as performances by traveling musicians.

There were plans in the making to offer a Permaculture Design Course, (PDC). It would start by being offered only on weekends from late spring through the end of autumn. As soon as Chaz said he'd be co-teaching that PDC, the idea of my assisting him arose.

A bubble of joy filled my chest. I could imagine myself mentoring students through the more difficult aspects of the gardening classes and see myself as an additional farmhand the CSA project folks had been asking for. As an added bonus, there was a school for local Deaf students in the nearest town, where I'd need to travel often to shop for staples and do my laundry.

It all sounded so wonderful—and was so obviously right up my alley—that of course I said "yes." Chaz recommended I become an exploring member of the community over the winter. (An "exploring membership" allows prospective members to test out what might be a mutual fit.) And as if all that weren't enough, there was also a yurt available as temporary housing! "I'll take it," I told Chaz. "I'll be there in a week."

The Final Frontier?

After arriving, I went for a tour and an interview. I had packed enough necessities to carry me through a 9-month sojourn, the kind of gestation period I thought would give me a large enough taste of their exemplary project. It all seemed so magical! I assumed I would be accepted by the founding group and further suspected that this could become a place I might want to settle more permanently.

For the rest of the winter, I rented one of four insulated yurts that had been erected on platforms built in a small clearing near the community center. Vanna, one of nine founding members was in charge of managing residency in the canvas yurts. Chaz lived nearby in a rustic cabin built with wood from the hillsides and harvested by horse loggers. (Several of my new acquaintances, including Vanna and Liam, would later become the support team for my not-yet-imagined pregnancy.)

Vanna was a clay artist and had hosted cob-building workshops to teach and assist in the building of her adobe-style cabin. The walls of cob homes are made with a mixture of clay soil, sand, and straw. These raw materials were readily available from the land and/or locally and required manual labor. The ecovillage training center network of organizers had promoted Natural Building as part of the wide variety of workshops facilitated by both community members, local homesteaders, and supporting members of the wider bioregion. Plenty of people were plugged in to the exemplary unfolding project.

Liam lived in a train caboose that he'd renovated into a cute tiny-home tucked into the forest.

I felt so lucky that this small group of creative people were to be my hosts, my neighbors, and now new friends on that lush and welcoming land! I had instant community and felt welcomed into this hospitable scene. We were a tight-knit group of visionaries carving out complementary and shared dreams. Chaz and I soon rekindled our romance.

Vanna told me about the magical journey of finding the land, and I heard others tell pieces of the story about how the founders had come together on this project. She also told me the story of her adoption. When she was small her adoptive parents told her she had come from a monkey tribe that suddenly descended upon the town, making themselves at home, running up and down rooftops, inside buildings, even swinging from chandeliers. They created such a ruckus they were chased out of town, leaving Vanna sitting alone in the dust. She had been looking for that tribe for years, with repeated disappointment. For her, co-forming community was like building the family network she always wanted.

As I was getting settled in, I was able to land a seasonal teaching job at the school for the Deaf, teaching science classes to high school students. I was able to bring them to the ecovillage on field trips. When spring came, they learned about the different aspects and sequences of growing food organically through their own hands-on experience.

I had also joined the local food co-op and volunteered there once a week for a few hours after work. My network from knitting together my work with the Deaf community and sustainable lifestyle was coming together beautifully.

Building a Cabin

When the growing season started in April, I had to give up my yurt to the original garden crew, so I moved into a tent. I was used to camping but looked forward to living in a more solid home. When summer came, Liam and another carpenter, Mike, helped me build a cabin from locally harvested wood. I found windows I could recycle, damaged sheetrock I could refurbish, and a special kind of insulation that had been manufactured from recycled denim. Chaz helped me tear out oakwood flooring from an old building in town that was being renovated.

This building project helped me feel closer to my dad, who was the contractor on so many buildings in his lifetime. I gained a lot more respect for the skills he had learned and practiced through the years.

The cabin, a 450-square foot hexagon, including a loft, was heated by a Jotul woodstove. A two-burner propane cookstove sat on the pinewood countertops in the small kitchenette area of the first floor. Chaz built shelves and Vanna sewed curtains. A few low wattage lights that gave me light for about an hour were powered by a small solar panel that had been installed on the roof. I had candles and kerosene lanterns when I ran out of power. Outside the front door was a well-designed water catchment system that caught rainwater in gutters and guided it to a cloudy storage barrel made with a thick plastic. There was also a spring water tap nearby where I could gather fresh potable water for drinking and cooking. The back door opened onto a deck overlooking a gurgling creek.

At the end of a day spent digging garden beds, and in order to celebrate the completion of my cabin, I warmed up leftover squash soup and opened a bottle of organic wine for Chaz and me. We ate under the moon, sitting on the deck, listening to the creek's song.

"I could live here forever," I whispered. Chaz didn't hear me. He would have rolled his eyes. He was willing to help me get settled, but wasn't too keen on my independence, hoping I might shack up with him instead.

Finding My Niche

I had a good track record after my first year of teaching Deaf high school students. That enabled me to inspire the school administrators to allow me to start the school's own organic garden. I was excited to help the students learn to harvest healthy food for school meals. This blossomed into merging with a summer camp program with an organic garden woven into the other activities. The school could see the value in having a program that could offer horticulture therapy as part of the design. I continued my involvement on several fronts: teaching organic gardening, harvesting, and cooking.

Through a community education program in town, I also taught an ecological health and wellness class called HEAL (Healthy Eating and Living). Students from these classes often came to help in the garden at the School for the Deaf. The Deaf students sold their organic vegetables at the local farmer's market.

When we put the gardens to sleep after the fall harvest, I was free to explore my desire to volunteer in Belize over the winter.

Through all of this, Chaz and I were so busy with our workday lives that, when we got together, we were always tired. I loved sitting back in the evenings to decompress from the day. While Chaz wanted to add marriage and family to this equation, I dodged his subtle inquiries, feeling more interested in continuing with the free and independent lifestyle I had carved out. I had found my niche and a home base that would serve me well into the foreseeable future.

Return to Belize

Chaz and I traveled together on my first trip back to Belize. We spent a month working with the now well-established Permaculture Project in the same Mayan village we had lived in during our college internships. I got reacquainted with many deaf people—the children more grown up than when I had first met them. Remembering that other deaf people were spread out among the nearby rural villages with minimal opportunities for education, I scoured the area to find them. I saw that many still stayed at home, learning the basic skills of sustenance, sustaining themselves by mimicking what they saw in the routine of daily living chores. Boys learned to trap food, farm, harvest, and build thatch-roofed homes; girls learned to plant rice, beans and corn, and tend the fields, then harvest, process, and cook the food. They also learned basketry and weaving. Without electricity and running water, people made do with what they had. Those villagers were jacks-of-all-trades. I was inspired but also saddened to witness their hardships.

As I had seen previously, deaf kids were still left out of conversations with their families and often sat isolated in their classrooms. The village school had been started by a church group that provided some ongoing volunteer personnel. It was managed by locals but, with a volunteer turnover from year to year, the teaching staff was both inconsistent and often untrained. For kids who needed really skilled support, the educational system was sorely lacking.

I met a new family with seven children, two of whom were deaf. Their teenage deaf son had missed out on things for so long that he became little more than the village clown. He didn't pick up on any of the sign language I tried to teach him; instead, he stayed with his minimal, rudimentary gestures.

His five-year-old sister, on the other hand, was ripe for learning.

I taught her ten or eleven signs and had her repeat them back to me. Her father watched with rapt attention to see her communicating with her hands. I voiced the words as I demonstrated the signs and she copied me: "Tree, house, eat, sleep, star." I pointed at her parents, signing "mother, father."

Her dad looked at me in disbelief with tears in his eyes after she signed "father." He asked, "You mean she isn't dumb?"

I said, "She is smart and, yes, she can learn."

He asked if I would return to his village to help the deaf people and their families, and I promised I would.

All too soon it was time to go back to the States so I could follow through on commitments at home. Chaz and I had enjoyed the projects we worked on in the village, though we hadn't seen each other much. On the plane ride home, we shared stories and reflections. I told him I had decided to start a new project: I wanted to open a small school for deaf children in the Mayan village. It would be specific to their needs. I was hoping to tuck the project under the arm of the ecovillage's educational nonprofit.

I networked with folks in Belize to build a team for this project. Over the next year, I found sponsors to support it and finally procured a small, abandoned brick building that had been built by the local army as a teaching exercise; it would be perfect as a one room schoolhouse for deaf students.

People from the Mayan Permaculture Project offered to let me use their bus to transport kids from nearby villages. A lodge used for weekend tourists was available during the week for kids who lived further away. Parents would pay me in rice, beans, and corn.

With financial support from sponsors I had recruited, mostly from the States, and the small amount of money I got from renting out my cabin half the year, I could afford to run the school.

Everything was coming together. I was developing a two-week experiential training program for Deaf students to be held at the ecovillage, some of them coming to explore internship possibilities with me in Belize. My plan was to recruit students from this training, those who could live without electricity and plumbing, to travel back to Belize with me once I was able to get the school opened.

Voila! I was settling into Shangri-La.

15
Detours

LIFE BACK AT THE ECOVILLAGE in Virginia was full in its own right, with my continued work in the community garden. I was also still overseeing the seasonal organic garden at the School for the Deaf, although I had stopped teaching classes there and started finding freelance interpreting work in town. Some people would say, "Oh cool, what a great new job. You're an Interpreter for the Deaf."

I would remind them, "I am an Interpreter for anyone in the conversation, both Deaf and hearing people." Sometimes it takes people a little time to understand that.

The new interpreting job was fun. It gave me the flexibility to work around my erratic schedule, juggling the complexity of the demanding (but still exciting) tendrils I was so good at sending out.

I liked people to know that there wasn't enough downtime in my home life for marriage and family. Why were so many people trying to encourage me to take that route? I brushed all that off, still jazzed by everything I was doing, as I continued to guide the growing project in Belize.

Friends in Town

Through the volunteer position at the food co-op, I was always meeting new people. In this sometimes-small world, Peter, the dance leader, whom I had met at the Maine Country Fair a few years earlier, was one of the best surprises. Peter, Christine, and Harry, the folks whose names I'd heard on Peter's answering machine years earlier, were moving to the area. Peter had landed a job managing the food co-op.

I was dating Chaz and almost instantly found myself attracted to Peter again, wondering what his connection to Christine or Harry might be. (I learned later that Christine and Harry were Peter's close friends, not his family.)

In confusing moments like this, my attention often returned to the train tracks that ran through town. I would go to sit and listen to the soothing sound of the wheels along the track and the intermittent blast from the train's whistle. It felt as though it was trying to tell me something, though I didn't yet know what. Even when no trains were going by, I could *hear* and *feel* the hum of the train in my bones. Early memories of sitting beside the train tracks with Dave would pull at my heartstring.

Meanwhile, Angela, my coworker and friend at the food co-op, whom I had met soon after moving to the area over a year ago, got some very disappointing news. I had witnessed her in the process of trying to adopt a child during that whole time, and now, with her being single, she was told there was almost no chance of her getting to adopt a baby. She preferred a baby so she could start them off on "a clean slate."

Circling Back to the Baby Offer

My heart went out to Angela. That's when I decided to offer to have a baby for her, a child she longed to raise, and who would be loved deeply. *Was there anything wrong with proposing such a gift?*

When I told Chaz what I had offered Angela, he was upset. "What am I going to tell my mother, Samantha?!" he shrieked. "Why don't we have our own children and raise them in the ecovillage? Dammit, girlfriend! And what about the gay guy from India you said you'd marry so he could stay in the U.S. until he could marry his boyfriend? Don't you know when to stop?!"

I had never seen Chaz this angry. His handsome face turned red with rage, and the veins stood out on his neck.

"Chaz, you already have kids," I said plaintively. "I know you really want to marry and have more, but I've seen you go through hellish parental triangulation in raising your two boys. What about the planet? Haven't you had enough?"

Chaz knew I didn't want to be tethered down with kids. I loved my freedom. Because of this impasse, we ended up breaking up while attending a weekend event with many of our beloved friends. They were surprised to see us end our sweet romance.

"I'm sorry Chaz. Please forgive me. Thank you. I love you."

Heartthrobs

One evening during this same event, as I walked alone to the fire circle, I spotted Liam, my tall, dark-skinned, brown-eyed, Vietnam vet neighbor. He had the kind of muscles that come from hard work—ropey, thick, and beautiful. When he smiled, his eyes almost disappeared, wrinkling into little half-moons of happiness. He smelled clean and fresh as spring-and he was so handsome!

I was so busy admiring his beauty, paying no attention to the path ahead of me, that I tripped over a stone at my feet.

"I should watch where I'm going," I muttered.

Liam smiled and the blaze coming from his face felt like the sunrise to me. He put his hand in mine and helped me to my feet. "Ya better watch your step, honey." Then he blew his train whistle. We laughed and hugged, enjoying our lighthearted connection.

Liam was an amazing storyteller and a good listener as well.

He helped me lick the wounds I felt over my breakup with Chaz and move on. I had done the same for him. For brief moments throughout our friendship, I thought I would fall in love with him, but I had seen too many women hot on his trail. That kind of competition wasn't for me. I thought it best to keep our relationship the way it was, since by then we'd become a little like brother and sister.

Peter showed up at the gathering with lithe and lovely Christine, her golden curls bouncing to match her bubbly demeanor. Harry was to join them later.

Peter began leading a circle dance and I remembered how much I'd loved dancing with him in Maine. My heart sank as he danced with Christine. At that time, the nature of their relationship was still a mystery to me, nor could I bring myself to ask.

In a circle dance, everyone dances together. Peter and Christine, Harry and Christine, Harry and Peter—who was with whom? I felt jealous of all of them. They had a special union, a connection, a family, and I had...what?

Choosing a Sperm Donor

Back in town, conversations with Angela over the next few months flowed beautifully. We became serious about looking for a donor. We looked at our friend pool, seeking someone who might be available to donate sperm while remaining open to giving the baby over to another family. Breeding a baby meant using exquisite care in who we would choose. Some of our specifications included someone who was intelligent, sincere, trustworthy, who cared about people and our planet, and had values aligned with ours. We hoped to find such a man in the body of a healthy, 30-something freethinker.

My ecovillage friends were pretty much open and adventurous. I got two offers from men in the village who were willing to donate sperm and another from Ralph, a CSA garden member from town.

I interviewed them all and shared the results with Angela. We agreed on Ralph. As it happened, he had applied to be a sperm donor years earlier while he was still a university student. He shared with us some information about sperm donorship we found useful. Since he had yet to father a child, our invitation intrigued him. And because I was not romantically attracted to him, he seemed a safe candidate. Our connection would be impersonal and businesslike.

Tying Up Loose Ends

We all weren't quite ready to move forward. I was working on opening a small school for deaf kids in Belize, looking for more members to sponsor kids there and seeking American volunteers to train for that work. Angela was likewise busy with her job and community involvements. We decided to put the whole idea on the back burner while I geared up for the next phase of my project and would be traveling out of the country.

I had more groundwork to do to get the school off the ground, so I set off on a short trip back there. I was still in the middle of launching the nonprofit's partnership with the country's agency on special education. It might take a few more years, especially with my anticipated pregnancy thrown into the mix, but I remained determined to do it all.

Solidifying My Birth Team Support

When I returned to the U.S., my newly-formed birth team eagerly awaited my arrival. Angela, Ralph and I met to continue planning for my impregnation and continued to explore the kind of connection we could imagine for the future.

We began to formulate written agreements that grew from our conversations. There was no template for this, nor did we realize how naive we were on the subject. We trusted one another and, at the same time, wanted some general written guidelines we believed we could uphold.

Angela referred me to a friend of hers, an adoptive father, so I could get some additional perspective. We had only one conversation before he insisted I connect with his friend, the birthmother of his adopted daughter. Though I did call her, I had had so little knowledge of the adoption process or the feelings of birthmothers and adoptive parents that I didn't know what to ask. My questions, therefore, were both shallow and brief.

The birthmom shared that she'd had some initial separation trauma and admitted it was a death of sorts but said she had made the right choice. When she'd given up her child, she already had other children. Thus, when she found herself with an unplanned pregnancy, she was open to relinquishing the newborn to a couple who were longtime friends of hers. She knew of their struggle to get pregnant, and here she was about to have another baby she hadn't planned on. It all seemed to have worked out well for them. I found it pretty intriguing. With that conclusion, I thought I had done my homework.

Peter, my dream boyfriend, had broken up amicably with Christine while I was away. We found ourselves drawn to one another. He was also from a large family and had no plans to have children of his own in this lifetime. He was excited about being of support to me on this journey. As for me, I was thrilled to finally have found a boyfriend who really understood and shared my feelings about children.

Some women in the ecovillage doubted my ability to separate from a child after its birth. The concerns they tried to share with me just didn't register. My conviction was strong. They hadn't grown up with so many brothers and sisters. They hadn't had to carry the number and kinds of responsibility I'd been burdened with. Who did they think they were trying to convince me with their stance? Most of all, why would they try to steer me to a path other than the one my brilliant plan had already created? I was highly offended.

I decided to meet with Harry, hoping he might give his heartfelt blessing to my plan to bear a child for my friend. A minister, Harry had become a generous member of our CSA project, supporting our education programs and sometimes mediating conflicts.

Living in community makes it hard to isolate oneself or hide from one's shadow side. The Chinese character for *conflict* means *opportunity* and *challenge*. The community was committed to using resources to create and nurture a healthy social fabric in all aspects of our lives. I listened to community members who were concerned with my plan, but I didn't listen to any advice that didn't fit my determination. I found Harry inspiring and wise, and with his blessing I was ready to move forward.

16
The Contract and Creating Life

AFTER OUR BRAINSTORMING, dialogues, and writing up draft agreements, Angela, Ralph, and I endorsed our cooperative contract on an open adoption plan. We believed that this contract would supplement the official legal documents, after realizing the state laws were too limited in giving us a framework to achieve our shared goals. In conclusion, we felt pretty well set with our mutual intentions, expectations, and agreements.

It was our intention to interact in ways that would provide the best environment for our child's growth and development. Angela would have full parental rights. Ralph and I would have limited rights of input and visitation, but we trusted that our mutual values would allow for flexibility, respect, and ease of communication.

Our contract basically reinforced the understanding that Angela would be the ultimate decision-maker, while Ralph and I would be supportive caregivers. We agreed to be available for as much (or as little) time as Angela would call on us, within loose parameters. We also agreed to follow consistent parenting guidelines as chosen and directed by Angela. She, in turn, would welcome our input on critical decisions, but she would retain the final say. We also agreed to be available for mediation should we run into unsolvable conflict.

Just as my friend June had done for the son she relinquished, I agreed to supply breast milk for at least the first three months of the baby's life. Angela agreed to travel with me during the baby's first year to introduce the baby to both sets of biological grandparents: mine in Maine and Ralph's in New York.

In addition, I expected to have visitation rights one day a week whenever I was in the country and to have up to two weeks a year to take the child to see my family at an appropriate age and developmental stage. Ralph expected to have the child one weekend a month, starting when the baby was about a year old, we thought. These visits would not be supervised and could involve travel, if that was agreed upon ahead of time.

Finally, we agreed that, in the event of Angela's demise or inability to function as a parent, Ralph and I would have legal parental succession before any other family members, though we would also maintain such family relationships as might exist at that time. Should Angela pass away, Ralph and I agreed to become co-parents and share custody of our child.

We finalized the contract with Angela's immediate family members, so we could feel reassured they understood and supported our plan. We then registered the agreement with the Register of Deeds. Everything seemed so well-thought-out, so official, so smart and businesslike.

If Only I Had Known

We did not recognize our own naïve ignorance. We really thought we had everything under control. It was only many years later, at an annual American Adoption Congress Convention, that I learned open adoption agreements don't hold water. The adoptive parents can cut off ties with the biological family at any time, no matter the reason, and with no legal recourse for the birth family. Sometimes this dissolution is necessary to protect children from being torn between two worlds.

In a support group for birthmothers at that convention, I met some of the mothers who had experienced that terrible, sudden severing of the bond they had built with their child. I saw the sadness and misery they carried, how it weighed them down and blocked their feelings of joy. These mothers expended so much energy into blocking their pain, only sharing it in support circles where others would understand. Though some had been able to reunite with their birth children once the child turned 18, these reunions tended to re-traumatize the adoptee. With deep, intrinsic loss of trust, the relationship could easily get severed again.

There are activists fighting strict laws that terminate birth parents' rights. These legal battles are led by adoptees who regret not having had the chance to know their birth families until they turned 18—if they could even find them after all that time. The American Adoption Congress works in part to help adoptees gain the right to their original birth certificates.

Every story has its own unique twists, but with the information helping them identify and find their birth parents, adoptees have a greater chance of discovering their biological identity. Such information about birth parents has historically been concealed to greater and lesser degrees.

Ignoring the Signs

Hopeful, idealistic, and naive, we went on our merry ways, trusting ourselves and the process we had created, believing ourselves worthy of the lofty agreements we made. The truth is that, while contracts are effective for careers, copyrights, and loan agreements, the process of procreation and its biologically driven aftermath are much more complex than any contract can cover.

Fertile Murtle

The next step in this arrangement was getting pregnant. It helped that years earlier, to avoid getting pregnant, I took a class that taught me about my own fertility cycle. This contraception method was more natural and much more reliable than the "Rhythm Method" my parents used, which skipped some of the more intricate steps. I had been tracking the length of my monthly cycle, measuring my daily vaginal temperature, and following each of the other steps on my list. Fortunately, my monthly periods were regular and predictable, as was the rest of my monthly cycle. I had a conscious awareness of when I was most fertile.

My first successful impregnation took place on a warm spring day in my unfinished cabin at the ecovillage. I lay in the loft, my cozy nest for the moment. I could hear the nearby creek singing from my futon on the loft floor. Ralph knocked on the door and reached up the staircase to hand me a syringe full of living sperm. We winked at one another, gave each other a thumbs-up, and then Ralph left me in privacy. I undressed from the waist down, lay back down, got myself situated comfortably, and then inseminated myself. In two weeks' time I tested positive for pregnancy.

Miscarriage

Three months into the pregnancy the unexpected happened. I was surprised at how emotional I became when the fetal heartbeat couldn't be found, and we were told that the pregnancy was no longer viable.

Follow-up with an ultrasound and a D&C procedure showed no clear reason for the end of this young life. I was heartbroken and needed to heal my body and my spirit.

Vanna brought a visiting Hopi elder to my cabin. With my permission, he performed a healing ritual for me, first burning sage to clear any negative energy. As I lay back, he circled his palms above my stomach as if gathering invisible energies, then he balled that energy tightly in his hands making fists. Raising his long arms towards the heavens, he opened his hands upward, in this way returning that spirit back to God.

Before he left, the elder offered a name for the cabin. He called it the *Sipapu*, which is a small round hole in the ground inside a Kiva (a Hopi ceremonial space). It is believed that the first peoples of the world rose from that hole to enter the present world. We felt incredibly honored. The elder's guided ritual helped me grieve the loss of my first pregnancy.

Travel as Salve

I took a much-needed break during the next few months, traveling first to Maine, mostly to visit my friend June. As usual, we provided much needed support for one another. We signed for hours, cried on each other's shoulders, and then June braided my hair.

We walked to the train tracks together to sit in silence, our hands in our laps. I could feel June's compassion for my loss. By contrast, I'd heard my own family members say much too often that maybe it was a good thing I miscarried, and that it would "probably be better to move on." This was so disappointing to me and so painful that I couldn't wait to leave my family roots.

Vanna had been traveling to India for years and convinced me to travel with her. "We'll do some eastern prayer rituals, take a dip in the Ganges, see the beauty of the Himalayas…clear your head."

It didn't take much to convince me to heal in this way. I enjoyed a month of exploration in both India and Nepal.

Then I traveled back to Belize for a few weeks, focusing on maintaining the momentum of my project aimed at servicing deaf students and their families. I set realistic timelines for opening the school. Things were moving along. I felt healed.

The Dream

Liam, Phyllis and a few others from the ecovillage had been traveling in Belize when I got there. We decided to meet up at a Mayan ruins for a Spring Equinox ceremony.

There, we were welcomed into a ritual circle where there hadn't been any ceremony for 500 years. The theme for the event was *fertility*. A native Shaman called in the energies for re-establishing celebrations at this site, while new life was breathed into that sacred ground with prayers, songs, and the burning of copal, a sweet-smelling tree resin. That scent brought back memories of growing up going to Easter mass. Copal was burned during the mass.

I set my intention of calling in another spirit, praying for a connection between my soul and the soul of a new life hovering in the wings, eager to come to our planet.

That night, a vivid dream accompanied my sleep. I saw myself sitting beneath a tree that was breathing as a human does. The vines growing up its trunk seemed like the veins and arteries in a body. Though my eyes were shut, I saw and felt myself floating within a vivid red cloud. I knew that cloud to be a very deep love that totally enveloped me. I never wanted to open my eyes again; I yearned to exist forever in that bliss.

Nothing else mattered. Being transported to this amazingly beautiful realm in a never-ending, timeless space, was totally magical. I could stay there and die, and I wouldn't even notice the transition. Was this the ecstatic feeling at the moment of death? Where was I exactly? Had I been transported to a place between worlds?

I found myself having a telepathic conversation with what seemed to be another presence in the room. I asked that presence why it would even want to come to earth when there was *that*.

They told me that, if they didn't come, they couldn't bring that love to the world, and so I said, "Come." and our hearts locked into one. The dream slowly faded, but I carried its magic into my morning, as if I had been initiated. I felt I had been granted permission to procreate. I knew there was an angel in the wings, ready to occupy my womb.

Pregnancy

I returned home to Peter's loving arms. He said, "I'm ready to fly, Samantha." We shared the excitement, and I was happy he would be accompanying me in the next chapter of my life. Angela was prepared for another go.

Once I felt settled, I plotted out when I would be fertile. This time, I wouldn't need to inseminate myself; Peter could do it.

Ralph knocked on the cabin door and handed Peter a syringe filled with dancing sperm and a salty teardrop and then went on his way. Peter handled the syringe, and our baby was conceived with love in the same nest as the first time.

To our delight, we got the positive pregnancy news within ten days. My due date was the Spring Equinox—one year to the date after I had participated in the fertility ceremony in Belize.

It was a typical pregnancy, starting with morning sickness every day for the first three months. During that time, the mere thought of the vegetarian fare that used to taste so good could now make me feel like vomiting. I became a carnivore once again. About the only foods I could get down were meat and milkshakes.

I read books about the growth of the embryo then the fetus. I gave pictures to Angela showing the stages: first the development from head to rump, followed by the hands and feet, along with the heart, brain, and other organs.

After week nine, the genitalia began to form. At week twelve, I went for a scheduled ultrasound. Because there are so few surprises, we decided not to learn the gender of the baby. My midwife gave me an envelope containing the ultrasound picture inside, just in case curiosity got the better of us.

Angela and I went to childbirth classes together. We were full of curiosity and a building anticipation as the months passed. I was aware of every new milestone our fetus passed, and yet I remained oblivious to the deeper bond that was developing right along with him or her. The midwives watched this process with both anticipation and trepidation.

By seven months, it became more difficult for me to live in my rustic cabin. To avoid climbing stairs to get into bed, I moved the mattress of my futon from the loft to the first floor, right beside the wood stove and its warmth.

My bladder was scrunched by my bulging uterus. Lacking indoor plumbing, I would fill a makeshift chamber pot with that liquid gold then often have to go out into the cold night air to pee again.

On starry nights I felt glad that my biological impulses would take me outside. My garden loved the nitrogen, but squatting became increasingly difficult for me. Trips to town for laundry and grocery runs also became more and more cumbersome.

Moving into Town

Knowing that I would be spending a considerable amount of time in town, I put a down payment on the purchase of a new townhouse, using my hard-earned savings. It had been under construction, following a timeline similar to that of my developing fetus.

I had kept my eye on the progress of the townhouse project and luckily there were a few units left. The wet weather had delayed the final phase of construction so it might take a month or so to close.

I had plenty of other places to stay. Some friends were going away for a few weeks during the holidays, and I was invited to house-sit for them. Their offer came just in time and was a great relief to me. Another friend needed a pet-sitter for several weeks. Then Harry left town and let me stay at his apartment. I also stayed for a while with Peter, but he needed his space, while I needed to nest.

Baby Em

I called the fetus "Baby Em." My beloved embryo. I had to keep this impersonal and not get attached beyond this stage.

Angela thought of baby names: *Maya Lynn* for a girl (for many reasons, including a play on the words *myelin sheath*, the protective coating of our nerves), and Lynn for a boy, from part of the biological father's last name. We learned that some cultures postponed naming babies until they were well into their first year of life. In those cultures, the waiting was to watch the baby's developing personality and give them a name that matched their temperament.

Once the baby was born we'd see how well the names we had chosen would fit. Our surprise couldn't wait though. We decided to learn the baby's sex during the seventh month of my pregnancy.

Angela imitated a drumroll. Then said, "The envelope, please."

I handed her the envelope containing the sealed ultrasound photo. I watched carefully as she opened it, studied the photo, grinned broadly and then squealed in delight, "It's a boy!"

I wanted to jump up and down but didn't want to disturb Em.

We still had 7 weeks left to go. It all seemed perfectly orchestrated. Slowly positioning themselves for the grand arrival were my friends Angela, Peter, Ralph, Vanna, Christine, and Liam, who had all been invited to be part of the birthing team.

Now you can see what led up to my journey into Motherhood.

Lynn Song, artist [9]

---

[9] When Lynn was 18, while I was working on this book, I asked him to draw a portrait of himself in utero. It was pointed out to me later that people who have an insecure attachment around the time they were born have difficulty drawing pictures of their mother, especially her face.

Part III
Summer 1997 – Summer 2003

Kyra Peregrine, artist

17
Kids Do and Say the Funniest Things

AGE ONE HIGHLIGHTS, beyond the typical caretaking routine that provided much entertainment, were Lynn's learning of sign language. I counted 175 ASL signs he knew before he was two. I would need to demonstrate this to you, and, since I can't here, just know this was a powerful and fun tool for us to have the ability to communicate before he could vocalize spoken words. While Lynn went through his terrific twos, fantastic threes, and onward, I was highly entertained, especially by his growing vocabulary.

Sleeping In

By not needing to rush off in the mornings, Lynn had the luxury and grew accustomed to waking up naturally on his own. He sure liked taking his time getting up, and often had funny things to say. When I returned to work, I didn't start until after the morning rush hour. If Lynn was still sleeping and I needed to turn more lights on to help him see to get ready for early preschool, he would quickly cover his eyes and say, "Stop that, it's too loud!" Or he might say: "My shoulders are awake, but not my legs. Come on, fast legs." One day after I had been up for a while, I walked back into our bedroom singing: "*Morning has broken, like the first mor-or-or-ning.*" He said: "I'm not broken, I'm just asleep." While getting dressed, he said, "My arms are peeking out of my sleeves," and, when putting pants on, said, "I don't want sleeves on my legs." On that day he wore one of my t-shirts made into a makeshift dress.

Mommy Mix-Up

On Lynn's third birthday, he got to spend his first overnight at his dad's. When we were getting his bag ready Lynn said, "Mom, there's room in the bed for dad to move in with us, okay?"

"Lynn, that could be interesting, but I don't think I would sleep very well. Lots of moms and dads choose to live in different houses and they create unique families. Want to hear a cool story about *you*?"

"A unicorn story?"

I took a deep breath. Was Lynn ready for this? "Hmmm...," I began, "Maybe we can think of a way to add a unicorn to your story. Unique means something special. Do you know you are special and lovable, and one of a kind?"

"Am I a unicorn?"

"You are unique. When you were born there was a big mommy mix-up. We were so confused, and I had a big sad feeling in my heart. I had been getting ready to work in a land far away and Angela was going to be your new mommy."

He clung to me, listening and looking into my eyes. "You wouldn't go far away, would you mom?!"

"No way! You know, a long time ago I wanted my brothers and sisters to be adopted because I didn't like taking care of them so much. Then when I grew up, I was too busy...," I didn't want to overwhelm Lynn and I wasn't prepared or knew what to say. "So, when the unicorn brought you from magic land...."

We both laughed and Lynn said, "I thought *storks* bring babies from the sky."

"Well, you are different, and I like to pretend that a unicorn brought you!" I tickled his armpits, and we laughed again.

"Is it a true story?"

"The part about the unicorn is 'let's pretend,' but the part about Angela is true because she loved you so much and she wanted to be your mama. But I loved you so much too, and I found out I couldn't live without you, so I told Angela she would have to find another special baby to love and guess who she found? Crystal!"

Lynn clapped his hands. "That was a good story, Mom! Say it again."

"Let's get ready for a unicorn to give you a ride to your dad's. I can tell you again when you get back." Lynn seemed satisfied with that, and I found time to sneak in a call to Ralph in order to let him know what I had told Lynn.

After that first night with his dad, we gradually transitioned Lynn to spending more time at Ralph's. Initially when Lynn was there, I felt the stirrings of an empty nest and had to keep telling myself I would have plenty of time to be with my "unicorn" son. I was surprised by how much I had enjoyed a domesticated life, and knew I would have to readjust once again, and get used to letting go.

Pure Fun!

To make the most of the transition with Lynn spending more time with Ralph, I made sure to use our time together to the fullest. We spent lots of time outdoors on long stroller rides, and we played at parks where he especially liked the monkey bars. Swimming was great fun. We both loved our walks to the railroad tracks.

One day, as we headed through a shortcut in some dense brush to go see the trains, Lynn said, "The tree is pinching me, and it has sharp teeth, Mom. Let's go the other way." So, we did. When we made it to the tracks, a train was passing by and Lynn said, "Look how the engine has strong muscles." Later, on the way home when he saw a water fountain, he said, "Stop here, I want to water my face."

At home, I often watched silently as Lynn played and talked with his collection of stuffed animals. He humanized them and made up dialogues, getting more sophisticated the older he got. I would find myself covering my mouth to stifle my giggles from the sidelines. George took a back seat to the giraffes, teddy bears, rabbits, and gorillas. Lynn had a lot of mother and baby pairs, and he ceremoniously walked them two by two into his toy Noah's Ark. It distressed Lynn that the only creature he lacked was a match for George. Though George was still a very special companion, Lynn yearned to find a mama for him too.

Some days we did art projects; we colored, drew, painted, cut out paper and magazines, glued things together, and we even sewed. I allowed Lynn one hour of screen time each day, watching educational programs on TV, or fun kids' movies. I would also let him save up hours to watch a full movie.

I read to Lynn a lot; for sure before naptime and bedtime, and then some. He often memorized the words in storybooks before he learned to read. Once, we performed Snow White and the Seven Dwarfs for a handful of neighbors starring our housemates and a few friends. Lynn was the narrator, and without knowing how to read, spoke the story word-for-word as he flipped the pages. We were all completely amazed by his memorization skills.

Motherhood was giving me a wonderful vicarious experience. Maybe it is the natural way we reparent ourselves. I feel resonance with the adage: it's never too late to have a happy childhood.

School

At school, the teacher had asked if I read to Lynn all the time, wondering how he had gotten such a big vocabulary. I told her we went to the library a lot and I read him plenty of books, but he was also learning American Sign Language, an activity shown to enhance language learning. Lynn was picking up ASL from Brian and our Deaf friends.

I followed some of the Waldorf School's ways, focusing on letting the creative part of Lynn's brain develop, rather than teaching him to read too early. (When he was ready to read at age six, he took off, excelling beyond his years.) After school one day, we went to the library and found the doors locked, "Mom, open the doors with your keys."

Lynn's school schedule allowed me a bit of freedom so I could get back to more of my freelance interpreting jobs, taking work between his school hours. I had already added some evenings and weekends while he was with his dad.

Housemates

We always shared our house with roommates. And living in a bilingual house naturally gave Lynn versatility in both English and ASL and an understanding of another culture. He learned how to associate with different kinds of people early on, as housemates came and went. The gift of the presence each person graced us with, for as long or as little as they lived with us, was always a blessing.

We had fun times cooking together with Phyllis and Brian, making big messes in the kitchen. Lynn seemed to enjoy dropping eggs on the floor. "Whoops, mom, it dropped by itself again," he would tell me, his hands covering his mouth in surprise.

"Whoops, Lynn, now *you* get to learn how to clean sticky, slimy, gooey eggs off the floor. It'll be so much fun and I'll be happy to help."

When Phyllis moved out, we said our sad goodbyes while knowing this wasn't the end. She would only be an hour away at the ecovillage and come back to town to shop. We went to look at her empty room. "Where did the bed go mom?" Lynn asked.

I said, "What do you think happened?"

"It flew away."

"And where did Phyllis go?" I asked.

"She flew away too," he said.

I wondered if he got that idea by watching the birds build their nests outside our cabin and later flying off after their eggs had hatched and the babies flew off, leaving the nests abandoned.

Cabin Life

During the summertime we lived in our cabin at the ecovillage, where Lynn had more of the great outdoors to explore. He was exposed to a cycle of life that revolved around nature and learned to live with minimal creature comforts. Being without electricity or plumbing was no big deal for Lynn, but when he returned to school and peed outside, he got scolded. He quickly learned standard school playground rules.

One summer, after a weekend in town, when Lynn's dad was dropping him off at the cabin, Lynn ran up to show me his hand. "Look what happened!" he said, "Blood was coming out of my finger, and I think my brains were coming out too, but Dad fixed it, he promised me."

Laying outside on the ground that evening looking up at the sky, I said, "The moon is hiding behind the clouds."

Lynn said, "The moon is far away in the air. I can't touch it, but I can see it eating something."

"What is the moon eating?" I asked him.

"Clouds," he replied.

We lay there awhile, watching the moon eating the clouds, before heading inside, and then I said, "Hey, Lynn, speaking of eating, do you want me to read the story about Sam-I-Am after your bedtime snack?"

"Okay, but only if you don't make me eat green eggs and ham."

"I won't make you eat green eggs and ham, but how about some blue eggs?" I asked, while shaking my head "no" and smiling, because I already knew his answer. Then I grabbed his hands. Pretending to eat his fingers while looking in his eyes I said á la Dr. Seuss, "I'm going to eat you because I love you. I will love you in a boat, with a goat, in the rain, on a train, in a box, with a fox, in a tree. Yippee," I squealed.

"Mom, that sounds silly!"

As I carried him inside, I continued. "I will love you here or there. I will love you everywhere." I spun him around and plopped him on the bed. "Thank you, thank you, Sam-I-Am!"

After rereading *Green Eggs and Ham* for the umpteenth time, I said, "Good night, my silly boy."

Lynn said, "Good night, my silly mama." With a kiss and a hug, he dropped off to sleep.

My world revolved around Lynn's needs while my career was partially on hold. At least I had gotten my priorities right, and it felt good. Though I had always thought I was not cut out to be a full-time mom, I found the primary caretaking role came naturally to me. While rolling with the punches that life delivers, I was becoming a silly mama in the process.

What a luxury to spend our summers at the ecovillage, with all the vibrancy of a living immersed in an earth based sustainable laboratory.

Family Reunions

Once or twice a year we traveled to Maine to visit Gramma and Gramps, and also to spend time with my friend June. During those vacations we enjoyed reunions with oodles of family relatives. On Christmas every family was to bring just one gift for their child to open. With so many of us, there wasn't any expectation that the adults would buy gifts for everyone. But we did bring a wrapped recycled present, which we used in a white elephant gift exchange game we played. Each gift had some humorous meaning to it that had us laughing for a long time.

Our family reunions were precious to me, especially during the time when my father was in slow decline. He had become unable to pick Lynn up or read to him clearly, but Lynn could still sit on his lap and show Gramps the pictures in his books. He always got Gramps smiling from ear to ear.

I Need to Talk to Peter Pan

The next summer came, and it was an especially hot one. We didn't have air conditioning. One night Lynn said, "I just want to wear my body to bed tonight," so he hopped into bed naked. After tucking him in with a lightweight sheet, I read him a bedtime story, this one about Peter Pan. Then we shared kisses and hugged goodnight. I was in my office when I overheard him talking. I tiptoed to the bedroom doorway and heard him repeating: "I do believe, I do believe…"

"Hey Lynn," I whispered, "who are you talking to?"

"Shhhh, Mom. I'm waiting for Peter Pan, but we better take the screens off so he can come in through the window. I want him to teach me how to fly. And maybe he knows how old grandpas can magically get young again. Will you read that Peter Pan story to me again?"

The next morning, with his usual dislike of getting up, Lynn said, "I'm so desperate."

"What do you mean?" I asked.

"It means I'm dripping tired. I waited up all night for Peter Pan to talk to him about Gramps. Maybe he can take him to Neverland and make him young again. I'm getting kinda mad waiting for Peter Pan to show up."

I wanted to cheer him up. "Do you want to read some fun and magical poems?" I asked him. Picking up Shel Silverstein's *Where the Sidewalk Ends*, I read:

> *If you are a dreamer, come in…*
> *A hope-er, a pray-er, a magic bean buyer.*
> *If you're a pretender, come sit by my fire…*

I told Lynn I was a magic bean buyer, and we were going to have a fun and interesting long life together.

The Art Car is Born

One cold winter night, Lynn, George and I were in the car, on our way to have dinner with Angela and Crystal. The roads were icy, and the windows kept fogging up. Lynn was sitting in his car seat on the back-passenger side telling George a secret that seemed to be more giggles than words. I couldn't help smiling.

Suddenly, I saw a car heading towards us, doing 360s on the ice. I panicked, pumping the brakes as hard and fast as I could. In the flash before we hit, I was terrified as the other car sped closer to the back passenger side of our car. Was I going to lose Lynn again?

Fortunately, only the front ends of our cars collided, both vehicles jolting to a stop. We each stepped out of our cars on shaking legs, hearts pounding, as we went to inspect the damage.

I lifted Lynn out of the car seat with George in his arms. He wriggled down to see what had happened. Looking at the front end of our car with one of its headlights smashed, Lynn said, "The car got hurt but it's not crying, George. It's gonna be okay." Then, he stretched his arms up to me and said, "Mommy, hold you." It was such a relief to pick him up and hold him! I blinked back tears of relief, knowing I couldn't have borne another loss.

After exchanging contact information with each other, we all got back in our mangled but drivable cars and took off very gingerly. I clung to my steering wheel tightly, white knuckling it, as I slowly and carefully steered us home along those icy roads.

To make a good situation out of a bad one, and since my car was still operable, I decided to turn our Honda Civic into an "art car" rather than send it to the junkyard. I started hosting car-decorating parties. The first party was with Angela and her neighbors and a pack of kids. I brought paint, brushes, glue and beads to glue on the car. So began the transformation of that old jalopy into an item of genuine interest. Soon, it became a car of many colors. We called it our Art Mobile.

That summer, I drove the Art Mobile to a family reunion, where my sisters and brothers, nieces and nephews, parents and other friends added to the car's funky evolution. Everyone had a chance to add their handprints to the car, where they stood out like signatures.

Despite his weakened state, my father used his walker to hobble over and put his own handprints on the hood, right next to Lynn's footprints. I was touched and saddened, as I thought this might be our last time together with him.

In the process of saying our goodbyes, after Lynn survived being smothered with kisses and hugs, he got on his hands and knees to say goodbye to some pretty rocks. Then he insisted on bringing some back home with us. It took him quite a while to "choose three."

As we finally drove away, Lynn called out the window. "Goodbye!"

I wondered and asked, "Who did you just say goodbye to?"

"Huh?" said Lynn. "I was saying goodbye to the trees."

"Lynn," I chortled, "you are adorable!"

Back on the highway again, we started singing our favorite songs, especially the ones whose lyrics we'd gradually adjusted over time:

"You are my sunshine, my only moonshine, you make me laugh…you'll never know Lynn, how much I love you…" and "You're Popeye the sailor man…."

Lynn Song, artist (age 7)

I once again was living near the sound of the train. I could listen to the whistle as the train passed by, a soothing sound that always brought comfort to my soul.

I started getting together with Angela again, while our kids became deeper friends. We told them the mommy mix-up story and how we eventually figured out where everyone belonged. Lynn and Crystal called each other brother and sister. While we thought we were having one child, we had two children, and their unique destinies brought them together. All's well that ends well!

Sock Monkey Haven

A month after our move, we were invited to be in an art car competition. I strapped Lynn's stuffed animals, George included, to the top of the car. Later that day, the owner of the record shop across the street from the Art Mobile's parking spot stopped by to inquire about George. He explained he had a collection of more than 100 sock monkeys, and George had a number of unique features he'd never seen before. Then, very politely and almost apologetically, he asked if George might be for sale. I asked the guy for his card and said I would get back to him.

When I explained to the collector that George, the sock monkey he'd admired, actually belonged to my young son, he immediately invited us to meet the tribe at the *Red Heel Monkey Shelter*, home to the largest brood of sock monkeys under one roof.

When I got home, I told Lynn I had met a man who claimed to have a tribe of monkeys and he wanted to meet George. I reminded Lynn that Vanna had been trying to find her tribe, and maybe George also wanted to find his. Maybe we would find a mama for him.

Lynn responded saying we really *needed* to see these monkeys because what if some of them wanted to be in his play? Maybe a few could move to our house instead? Or at least before he let George live with that tribe of strangers, Lynn needed to be sure his good friend would be safe and happy and have lots of friends. And afternoon snacks too.

We set off for the Red Heel Monkey Shelter within the hour. Because it was George's nap time, on the drive over he lay curled under his own blanket in Lynn's lap. But no monkey could sleep through what greeted us!

Those monkeys at the Shelter had just about taken over the collector's house. They came in every shape and size you can imagine. Each monkey had its own name. All their costumes were clearly hand-sewn; no two costumes were alike. There were sock monkey ladies and gentlemen dressed for a 17th century ball. Some wore powdered wigs and others sported wild hairstyles. Some wore jewelry even though they were dressed for the gym; some wore bandannas while others wore gimme caps. We saw monkeys with monocles and monkeys with sunglasses. Some had short crew cuts and others had dreadlocks. These were not your ordinary, everyday sock monkeys. These monkeys had serious *style*.

While I kept on moving from one room to the next, Lynn remained in the first room, talking earnestly with the owner. As George's "big brother," Lynn took his responsibility for George's well-being very seriously. Before he could let George live with this fabulous tribe, he had to make sure of several important matters:

1. Would George find good friends to play with and talk to when he felt like talking?

2. Did the tribe's owner or another grownup live on the premises? A grownup had to be present at all times so George would always be safe. Lynn didn't want him to be scared.

Lynn and George had a brief conversation, and both agreed that this looked like a great and fun tribe for him to be part of.

"But let's just try it first to see if George likes it," he told the proud caretakers. "When we visit, if we see he is not happy, then we can bring him home, okay?" It was a deal. We said our goodbyes with mixed feelings:

"George, I'm sorry. Please forgive me. Thank you, George. I love you."

Grandpa's Death

The seasons rolled on, each in their own way filled with the delights of parenthood. At the end of another fun summer at the cabin, just after we packed up and moved back to town for the kindergarten school year, I picked up a message from my mother asking me to please call. She sounded sad! As soon as I got Lynn to bed, I dialed my mom.

"Samantha, honey, I've been trying to reach you. Why don't you get a phone in your cabin?" She was clearly very upset. "Your dad got sick earlier in the week. He knew you were coming soon, but the sudden illness hit him hard, and he couldn't hang on. He said to tell you: 'I'm sorry. Please forgive me. Thank you. I love you.' He passed away this morning."

I started to cry. My dad had been ill for a long time, living with lung cancer, and we knew he wasn't long for this world. But the suddenness and finality of it hit me deeply. Every time I had visited him, I had said my goodbyes not knowing if I would see him again. I was so disappointed not to be able to see him alive one last time.

Lynn was now five years old. I had been talking quietly and was muffling my words and tears, but he must have heard me. He got out of bed and walked over to me with his head hung low, tugged at my arm and asked, "What's wrong Mom?"

I knelt down and hugged him, and said, "Lynn honey, Grammy said Gramps wasn't feeling well this week and he asked Grammy to take him to the hospital. You know Gramps never complained and he never liked even going to the doctor. After Grammy got him ready to go, he sat down on the steps in their house, closed his eyes, and died peacefully. Remember when Beau died?" I hugged Lynn close. He was quiet, contemplating what it all meant.

Worried, he said, "Gramps was old, but my dad's not. *He's* not going to die, right?"

"Your dad will probably live a long time. He's like Superman. He's strong and takes good care of himself. He's a lot younger than Gramps and he doesn't smoke like Gramps did. Smoking made Gramps' lungs sick."

"Mom, I am never going to smoke."

"Promise?" I asked.

"Pinky promise. Cross my heart and hope to die, stick a needle in my eye."

"What?" I gasped. "Who taught you that crazy rhyme?"

"My teacher at school. And she taught me the pledge of elegance too."

"Lynn, you make me laugh! I need that right now."

We headed up to Maine for the funeral, driving through a rainstorm. On the way, above the sound of the pitter patter of rain on the car roof, we talked about death. I tried to explain. "When we see Gramps, it will look like he is sleeping, but his life energy is not in his body, so he will not be breathing. He will never wake up."

I paused to drive in silence as Lynn looked out the window noticing the interesting weather, "It is iceberging, Mama. Will Gramps feel the icebergs when he is buried in the ground?" he asked.

"Isn't it beautiful? It's called hail. After we say goodbye to Gramps and bury his body in the ground, his body won't feel anything because he is not in his body anymore. When we close our eyes, we can still see him, and we still feel him in our hearts."

"I can feel Gramps in my knee, Mom."

"In your knees?"

"No, in my knee. This one," Lynn pointed to his left knee.

I bobbed my head up and down in agreement. "If it hurts I'll kiss it when I get out of the car."

The funeral was held at the Catholic church my parents went to every Sunday. It was filled to the brim with relatives and friends from near and far. June walked up, escorting my childhood sweetheart Dave, their arms locked at the elbows. What a surprise!

June signed, "We love you, Samantha, and are sad and sorry about your dad's passing." The three of us held each other for a long minute.

I introduced Dave to Lynn, who was being shy and clingy, and explained that Dave was my old boyfriend and had Deaf parents. "He offered to interpret for the funeral so June can understand."

As I stood there, I was a little surprised when deep loving feelings for Dave welled up inside me. He was as handsome as ever, and I would have enjoyed connecting further with him, but there was no time. For a moment I wished that he was Lynn's father. Though I was longing for more interaction, I lost Dave in the crowd of reunited relatives and friends as the day's celebration of my dad's life unfolded. When I realized he had left without saying goodbye, I felt even sadder.

After the trip, it took weeks to give Lynn reassurance about our safety. He wanted us to go on a balloon ride far up into the sky. He believed that would be the place where we would never die. When we passed churches with stained glass windows he would say, "There's Gramps' church." When he heard a song on the radio with a high operatic voice, he would say, "It's a song for Gramps." At night we shared appreciations from the day and talked about what was on our minds and in our hearts. If the sad memory about losing Gramps was troubling Lynn, he would write a note to him and place it by his bedside. One night he said, "Tonight I'm gonna leave it on the top bunk for him to read in the night. It will be easier for him to reach it."

Growing Wings?

On another night we were reading *How to Get Along at School*. One rule was: *Pay attention*. I asked Lynn what that meant, and he said, "It means make sure you don't forget something, like putting your clothes on and being naked." The next morning, I told him not to forget that I would be picking him up. He would not be riding the bus back home. He said, "Don't worry, I have a rememberous mind."

When I picked him up, I asked how his day went, and he said, "Today a butterfly flew into my cup of water. It left some dust from its wings. I drank the potion fast and I think I'm gonna grow wings."

My heart fluttered. "I'll be watching them grow, sweetie," I said, with a big smile.

18
Thank You, Belize

I FELT IT WAS HIGH TIME I got myself back to Belize to get some closure. I had told the people in the village where I volunteered that I would be back and then I never showed up. I was afraid my written updates to them might not have reached them, and/or since many of them never had the opportunity to learn to read, they might not have found someone to read my letters. I wondered if they got the pictures I had sent. Sometimes with pictures at least they would get part of the story, and then they could use their imagination to fill in the gaps.

I had spent many winters traveling to Belize and it will always have a special place in my heart. It was there where I saw and experienced firsthand how people live in developing countries, often from hand to mouth, in substandard housing. In the rural Mayan villages limited food choices and supply cause them to have to ration their food so it will last until the next growing season. This is without the creature comforts of plumbing and electricity. Other needs barely get met. The village communities are ninety percent self-sufficient.

Somehow, they survive. The people's hearts are wide open; they help one another and share with their neighbors, generous with what they have. They will give you their last dime even if it means going hungry. One has to see it, smell it, taste it, hear it, feel it, to really understand it.

Re-entry after returning always hit me hard. We in the US are five percent of the world's population yet use twenty-five percent of the world's energy. Statistics about consumption show how gluttonous the US is. I do wish everyone could get to experience the kind of richness I found that money can't buy.

This dichotomy reminds me of what an old mountain guy said. He grew up very poor in the Appalachians. He said: "When I was young, we didn't have nothing, and we was happy. Nowadays people have everything, they want more, and they ain't happy."

Anyway, I was drawn to go back and at the very least share some of what I had experienced with my son, and was hoping June would join us. I wanted to introduce my friends there to my beloveds, and thank the villagers for inspiring me and for accepting me.

Passports Trigger Longing

Before Lynn's school year ended, I contacted June and invited her to travel with us over the summer. She was available! This would be her first trip out of the country since she'd been adopted from Korea as a five-year-old, and Lynn's first international trip as well, so we had to get passports.

When I mentioned to June that she could use her passport to go to Korea, she said that thought had immediately popped up in her mind. Our trip planning to a developing country opened up things she had buried and sparked lots of questions for both of us. We had never talked about her homeland when we were younger. It was like I was meeting a new person. I wondered if we should be planning a trip to Korea, too. For the first time she started talking about her birthplace. Feelings welled up and then lots of tears as she imagined meeting her birth family.

June was a birthmother too, and I already knew how the separation from her infant son had saddened her deeply. Despite being allowed to visit him once a month and her commitment to having some connection with him, those visits would open up a never-ending wound. Saying goodbye over and over was painful.

My own separation from my son at the beginning, even though it lasted only two and a half months, felt like an extremely miserable eternity! Did she want to find her biological mother? Did she wonder if she looked like her? Did she have siblings? And how were our children impacted? We had been told they were resilient.

We had opened up a can of worms but then had to put the juicy discussion we were having on hold to plan the details of our trip to Belize. The seed had been planted for future exploration into her roots.

Flooded with Memories

Lynn and I set out on our trip and landed in Belize within a few hours of June's flight. After going through customs with their rudimentary system of security, we grabbed our small backpacks, and happily found June who had been waiting for our arrival. We went to the currency exchange office with our American dollars and were all set. While walking out, I noticed the familiar face of a taxi driver I had ridden with years ago standing at the curb as if waiting for us! He remembered where to take us. Unfortunately, knowing nothing about Deaf people, he called the school I was visiting, "the school for imbeciles." It hurt me to hear him refer to it that way, and I gave him more accurate terminology for people who had varying special needs.

Riding from the airport, which was located on the outskirts of Belize City, we passed groves of palm trees, and a cluster of small, thatched roof huts, each with its clothesline of colorful garments waving in the wind, dotting the countryside. There were large metal rainwater catchment tanks for every dozen huts or so and people at water streams fetching water in clay pitchers. Lynn sat on June's lap while both had their eyes glued to the windows as a whole new world was passing by. Kids were running around naked, playing joyfully outside the small wooden shacks, kicking up dust. Lynn made his way to the front seat and whispered to me, "Where are the kids' toys?"

"Shhh, Lynn, I'll explain later." The car did not have air conditioning, and it was a hot, sunny day. We rolled our windows up and down, depending on which patch of dusty road we were on. Bob Marley's voice blared from the radio: *Every little thing's gonna be all right....* The warm wind blew welcoming kisses.

We spent the first night near the school where I'd administered all my previous work. The motel had no hot water (get used to it!) and no toilet paper. What it did have were cement floors and some friendly mice. It was pure sweet nostalgia being back!

Deaf Education

On our first morning we woke to the sound of roosters, and, after a quick breakfast of plantain, rice, and beans, we went to meet the superintendent of the school. She updated me by sharing that the man I'd been trying to reach, a former contact known affectionately as "the Father of Deaf education" in their country, had fled after a volunteer reported him for abuse. I also was told that he'd absconded with the funds meant to pay his employees' salaries.

I was heartbroken and shocked. My last contact with him was shortly after Lynn was born. I'd explained I would not be back for some time but was sending three volunteers. Now I was here to surprise him and introduce him to my son. It was terribly upsetting to hear what had happened, and my heart went out to all the people who had been hurt by him.

The years we'd spent working on programs to separate Deaf students from the other developmentally delayed kids was not all for naught. It had been successful in its own right. Although the Deaf program of the school had closed after the tragedy, it was clearly essential for the Deaf students to have their own classroom where they all could be together and help one another. Before long, a talented replacement teacher had been hired and the program revived.

Orphanage

After a few days of visits, it was time to head to the southern part of the country, where I had spent most of my time. We hopped a bus that was filled to overflowing, but we were able to squish in. For two hours, we stood in the aisle, passengers squeezing by us at every stop. June and Lynn tolerated standing in tight spaces with lots of body contact and body odor. I could see they were experiencing some culture shock in different ways and let them just take it in with no need for explanations.

Finally reaching our stop, and relieved to get off, we made a bee line to a café serving conch soup. We then visited the orphanage where Angela's daughter, Crystal, had lived. I couldn't help but wonder about the kids at the orphanage, what their stories were, and what their fates were. June was reflecting on her journey as an adoptee from a foreign country and her experience in placing her own child up for adoption. I felt so grateful that Angela had Crystal and that Crystal had Angela and that Lynn and I had each other. In the afternoon we caught the last crammed bus to Punta Gorda, for another six hours of exhausting travel.

With heavy feelings, after a good nights' sleep, we caught an old school bus (typical transport in these poor rural areas), into the jungle. It snorted and wheezed its way to the Mayan village where the Permaculture Project had flourished and where I had worked with families of Deaf children. Lynn was oblivious to all the ways June and I were feeling triggered. He brought welcome comic relief, especially when he mimicked the Howler monkeys' movements and sounds.

Reunions in the Village

We had many beautiful reunions during that trip. The first of these was with a family who lived in a two-room hut. Of their seven children, two were deaf. I introduced everyone to Lynn and June, and explained why I hadn't returned. I had sent numerous letters, but they never received even one. Letters are delivered by bus drivers who often can't read. Even if they did reach their destination, few adults in these villages were literate.

Framed pictures I had gifted the family years ago decorated the dirt walls of the hut. Seeing photos of these children sitting on my lap, so small then, and now so grown up, brought back many memories. Tears of sadness and joy filled my eyes.

June and I spent two weeks volunteering on various projects with the villagers. We hoed, planted, and harvested in their gardens. In the evenings we enjoyed black beans on tortillas made from scratch, prepared over a wood fire. After dinner we taught the family more sign language. Lynn went along with all of this activity without complaint, as if it was second nature. We also played Uno and Yahtzee, games I had packed that I knew almost everyone would be able to play using some basic signs language.

After dark, the room was dimly lit by candles made with animal lard, which we supplemented with light from our flashlights. The candles were valuable, so it was important for us to conserve both the lard and the batteries for other utilitarian purposes.

We three slept in hammocks that hung from the rafters alongside several of the older kids. The hammocks were strung out at bedtime above the dirt floor of the main room next to the cooking fire pit. The rest of the family slept on the only bed they had: a double-sized bed on a wooden platform. Their mattress was stuffed with straw and palm leaves. It was quite a cozy arrangement.

Those of us who could hear heard the marimba being played off in the distance at the local church. People gathered in prayer and song to bless the freshly harvested corn crop. They prayed that it would not meet the same fate as the previous year's crop, which had been infested with rats. Many of these villagers had lived on rice and beans for breakfast, lunch, and dinner all year long. As we drifted off, we could hear critters running around in the rafters, maybe mice but more likely scorpions. Though Lynn and I got used to it, I thought it was lucky for June that she couldn't hear them.

At the end of our time there, we found it hard to leave the village. Buses came only twice a week and left the village at 5 a.m., when it was still dark. We were off on another adventure, bouncing over the washboard roads, Lynn sleeping in my arms. I wept. June asked me what was wrong, and I told her not to worry. I was already missing those beloved villagers and didn't know when I would see them again. Dust filled the dry air and coated my face leaving tear carved trails down my cheeks. The closer we got to town, the more passengers filled the bus, eventually to double capacity. It was a bittersweet ride.

Tropical Playground

We made our way to the coast and by midday had boarded a small motorboat painted red, yellow, and green with "Hanna" painted on the side. "We gwaan" (hello), greeted our Rastafarian driver. He had beautiful, long thick black dreads, shiny white teeth (with a front tooth missing), and a smile to beat all smiles.

"Who is Hanna?" I asked.

"My mama, da one what she barren, but she pray and she pray for a son. When he come born, she name him Samuel and dat be me."

Samuel skillfully guided us across the choppy waters of the Caribbean, taking us to the island village of Caye Caulker. He unloaded our backpacks to a bicycle cab with a big cart welded to its frame. Our bicycle cabby took us to check into our hostel and waited while we changed into swimwear. He then rode us back to Samuel's boat for an afternoon of snorkeling. Several hours later, Samuel got us back to the island for dinner. As we said our goodbyes, he said, "Me a go, praise Jah."

"Praise Jah, Samuel," I said waving. He had no idea how much his mama's story meant to me.

In the evening, we walked the village looking for any Deaf folks who lived there. The few we did meet there had been isolated and thus never exposed to any sign language, unlike those on the mainland where sign language had filtered down through church groups. We found it harder to converse with these folks. We managed, however, using only rudimentary gestures and the few home signs they taught us. Nevertheless, we were able to teach them how to play the Yahtzee and Uno games we brought with us. Some things really are universal.

Farewell My Friends, Have a Good Life

After a few days of island leisure, we returned to the mainland to fly home but not without a heartfelt farewell. Having been in and out of this city several times, I had gotten to know a group of Deaf people, and they hosted a surprise party for us on our last night. I thought a few people might attend, but instead an overloaded pickup filled with old friends pulled up.

The truck tires looked almost flat with their combined weight! We had the same dinner we ate at most meals: fried plantain, rice and beans, and some of their own special alcoholic brew. A handsome young Deaf fellow was falling in love with June. She on the other hand was more realistic, knowing it was unlikely she would ever return.

On the airplane, each of us was quiet for some time as we integrated all the new interesting people and places we had just experienced. I hid my tears of sadness; this was one of the harder travel "good-byes." Lynn was busy drawing in his journal book.

At some point during that flight, June and I began talking about looking for her family in Korea. All her life she'd been curious about them, and after traveling in a foreign land, the desire to know them was stronger than ever. Because she had relevant identifying information, she already knew about the orphanage she had lived in. More importantly, knowing that her biological parents were Deaf meant that she had a good chance of finding them.

I looked over at Lynn, still busily drawing, and asked if he would draw something for his dad.

He continued his artistic endeavor for a short time and then said: "Look at my picture, Mom. The best thing I ever gave my dad was *me*."

Lynn Song, artist

19

Reunions

REUNIONS HAD BECOME a new theme in our lives. First, perhaps after overhearing me talking to June about her plan to search for her biological family, Lynn wanted to get George back from his sock monkey tribe at the Red Heel shelter. It had been over a year since we'd been there, but Lynn remembered the promise that any time he wanted him back, George was his, tribe or no tribe.

I went alone to inquire. My head hung low with the prospect of announcing that we were revoking the placement, but when I told them the story, they were elated. They said George had never bonded with his family and had been hoping Lynn would come back to get him. They took me into the next room where George was sitting next to a packed suitcase, evidently waiting for Lynn. My heart soared with relief!

We arranged a time for me to return with Lynn to pick up George and receive an autographed copy of their hot-off-the-press book, *Sock Monkey Dreams*. George's story was one of the features.

I could see that magic was in the air, even in the trickster ways it has of showing up. I saw that when it isn't obvious, especially when it takes so long to reveal itself, when you are just about ready to give up—lo and behold! There it is again: Magic!

On the day of the reunion, Lynn was ecstatic to see George again, hugging and squeezing him and singing, "George, I missed you so much! I'm bringing you home!"

June, Aka Jeong Sik Ko

Reunion was on June's mind, too. She had decided to continue the search for her birth family, and when we found out a neighbor of mine was hosting an exchange student from South Korea, she wanted to meet her.

When June met Marika, she felt an instant connection to this woman who reflected her own kin. This meeting felt like "home." Looking at a large world map, they were able to compare birthplaces. June told Marika about her family of origin. She recalled being told that her biological Deaf parents were too poor to raise her. While she was living in the orphanage and school for Deaf children, they visited a few times to see for themselves that she was well fed and enjoying being with the other children. June always assumed that her biological parents thought it best for her to have a family that could give her so many more opportunities than they could. Now she was hungry and ready to learn more about them.

After gathering all the adoption paperwork that fully disclosed her original name, birthplace, and the names of her biological parents, June attended an international conference in Las Vegas. There she met Deaf people from around the world, including a Deaf man from Korea. Using an ASL/Korean book of sign language, they managed to have a choppy, yet deeply connecting conversation.

She introduced herself to him as "Jeong Sik Ko," her birth name. He recognized her name immediately, with some shock and amazement. He said he knew her father, who had been looking for his long-lost daughter for many years. Of all the centers working with Deaf people in South Korea, *he* worked at the one nearest the orphanage where June had lived! They hugged in delight!

June stayed in touch with him after the convention. In less than a week, thanks to the internet, he connected her with her biological family. To facilitate communication with her parents in Korean Sign Language (KSL), June found a Korean-born Deaf woman living in Seattle to help. This woman had been adopted from the same orphanage. Years earlier, she had found and reunited with her Deaf biological parents as well as a Deaf brother. The woman had learned KSL on her visits to Korea. Using her as an Interpreter, June was able to make a three-way Skype call. In that way, she met her parents on the global highway of internet wizardry.

Over videophones in three different parts of the world the call was surreal and mind blowing. June's father took a long look at this unfamiliar woman claiming to be his daughter. The look on his face told her that he doubted her claim. He asked her to take off her glasses and when he still didn't recognize her, he thought this was just another hoax. For the last thirty years, this man had been searching for his daughter (eventually through the internet) and throughout that time, he'd been bombarded with scams from people claiming the reward he was offering. But then June mentioned a scar she'd had all her life.

"A scar? Where?" her father asked.

In reply, June lifted her shirt and pulled her pants down slightly to show him a scar at the top of her right buttock, that she had since she was a baby. "Here," she pointed.

He immediately recognized the scar from a fireplace burn. "Oh, my daughter, my daughter!" he declared. They were both overjoyed and in tears! Then he put his hand to the video screen, as if to touch her, and she followed suit, trying to somehow feel her father's touch. They stared at one another in disbelief. By the end of the conversation her father told her he would send June money for the plane and to please come as soon as possible.

With her passport ready, June was able to put the rest of her life on hold and make the trip to Korea. Her parents met her at arrival, along with a biological sister. All were dressed in traditional Korean clothing. Each held a bouquet of flowers for their long-lost member of their family. Journalists with TV cameras showed up to film this memorable reunion.

June soon learned that on a visit to the orphanage when she was six, her father had signed papers to release her for adoption without understanding what he was agreeing to. He had believed he was simply extending her stay at the orphanage. Her parents were too poor to have visited June and her two Deaf siblings and had rarely seen them. On that visit June's cousin had guided her father to sign the adoption papers only for June, since she was the youngest and thus the most sought-after by prospective adoptive families. On his next visit to the orphanage, he was horrified to discover that his six-year-old was gone. There was nothing her father could do about it and he was crushed by the loss. He had carried June's picture in his pocket for thirty long years, showing her face to so many people, asking if they had seen his daughter.

At an orphanage reunion in Korea, June was able to meet some of the other students who had been in her class all those years ago. Most of them had been too young to be able to recognize each other as adults, and they had to use class pictures to identify one another.

One Deaf man introduced himself, and then he pointed to a picture taken just before June's adoption. In the picture, a boy and a girl were signing to each other the universal sign for "I love you."

"This is you and me," he signed. "Can you tell?"

He had been smitten with her when they were both young. Now he found himself smitten with her all over again. What magic!

The fact that his parents were also Deaf, had made it much harder for him to find a life partner. That's because hearing parents usually don't want their Deaf children to marry another Deaf person for fear of having Deaf grandchildren.

Within that year June married this man and, to make the world smaller, June's interpreter for that first phone call with her family was her husband's sister! June legally changed her name back to Jeong, and now lives in Korea with her husband and their baby son.

Vanna's Long Search

Magic continued to reveal itself: this time in Vanna's search story. She had secretly tried to find her birth family for ten years before her adoptive parents died. Then it was another 25 years after their passing that she had continued her search in vain to reunite with her biological kin. It was a very old and tiring story for her. When her efforts still didn't result in any good leads, she hired a private detective to continue looking on her behalf. This led only to more dead-ends, familiar disappointments, and a wad of money spent to no avail. For the umpteenth time, she was feeling ready to give up.

At around this time, I was registered to attend an upcoming Adoption Congress convention in Denver, where I hoped to meet and personally thank the keynote speaker, Nancy Verrier. She was the trauma consultant who had helped me understand so much about adoption after Lynn was born. I convinced Vanna to join me because there was another keynote speaker whose topic was DNA searches. This actually was the next strategy Vanna had started using in her recent search attempt. She'd plastered her DNA results all over her dining room walls, but so far had been unable to find close matches to her DNA.

At one of the convention's support groups for adult adoptees, Vanna was blown away by others' stories of searching for their roots. These folks truly understood her plight. Two other support groups were woven into the convention agenda: one for adoptive parents and another for birth parents. I attended the one for birth parents. There, I too was blown away by meeting Mary, a "search angel," who helped adoptees find their biological families. I couldn't wait to introduce her to Vanna!

I was disappointed to learn that Nancy Verrier had a family emergency and wouldn't be there to offer her presentation on adoption separation trauma. Nevertheless, I did make an important connection with Mary.

She had a sad story about her reunion with a daughter she had given up at birth. After searching for each other for years and finally meeting, her daughter went away from their brief reunion with bitterness towards Mary for "abandoning" her. Despite Mary's attempts to explain what had happened, her daughter could not stop blaming her birthmom for the way her life had turned out.

Knowing that sometimes reunions do go well, Mary still wanted to help others reconnect with their lost families. In the process of finding her own daughter, Mary had learned how to be a search angel. She had since been plenty busy with clients from Texas. After twenty years of that good work, she was retiring. Until I introduced Mary to Vanna. They both stayed up all night talking and Mary, after listening to Vanna's long search and her request for help, thought she might be able to get somewhere with Vanna's DNA results.

Within six months, Mary was able to fill in all the gaps to uncover who Vanna's birthmother was and where she lived. The wait to know her had been interminably long but now was finally over.

After Vanna's initial and emotional phone call to her long-lost mother, she dropped everything and took a trip to Florida to meet her 94-year-old mother. It had been over 60 years since they had been together. Their tearful reunion was the happiest day of Vanna's life. Her mother took one look at her and said, "You've got my red hair!"

Her mother was alive and well living independently and still went out dancing. She lived near Vanna's half siblings but Vanna was not allowed to say anything about it to anyone. Despite the family resemblance, it hurt Vanna deeply when together at a party, she was NOT introduced as a daughter but as a photographer friend, there to take pictures. Vanna said nothing, guessing that her birthmom was too embarrassed to have to admit she had a child out of wedlock. She continues to visit her mother and get to know her siblings at arm's length.

"When mama passes, there will be more excavations, but not now," she told me. "At least I finally know where I began. You have no idea how big that is."

Resolution for Harry

Upon arriving back home, there was a letter from Harry, my minister friend who had been such a huge source of support after Lynn's birth. He wrote that he had finally connected with his long-lost daughter and was mostly focused on catching up with her. They were both so joyful to have reunited after 25 years of separation!

Crystal

I feel incredibly privileged to have witnessed these beautiful, healing family situations and to have heard so many life-changing stories. At the time of writing this book, Crystal has tickets to Belize. She plans to travel there this summer with her adoptive mother Angela. Together they will visit the orphanage where Crystal had lived so many years ago before they became a family.

20
Save the Gorillas

ONE DAY, OUT OF THE BLUE, I received a letter from Dave, my childhood sweetheart. It had been fifteen years since we'd been together and a few years since I'd seen him briefly at my father's funeral. I was taken aback to see his name on the envelope. Familiar romantic feelings welled up in me as I rushed home to open the card. It was a beautiful picture of colorful vegetables ripening in a lush garden. He had written a short note:

> Dear Samantha,
>
> I hope this finds you and your family in the best of health. I asked June for your address. I have thought about you almost daily since I saw you at your father's funeral. That was no time to try to catch up. It's been quite a stretch since we last really talked. I'd very much like to know more about how you're doing and what you're up to these days. I also want you to know that what we once shared together was deeply meaningful to me and to this day, remains.
>
> Even if you don't want to communicate further with me, perhaps you'd be kind enough to let me know that you have received this note.
>
> Sincerely,
>
> Dave

I was thrilled! If I was reading between the lines correctly, he was interested in some kind of exploration and, at the same time, would be respectful if I didn't want to go there.

I wrote back right away, telling Dave I was going to be in Maine in about six weeks with my six-year-old son and my friend Liam. Lynn's school would be out for the summer, and we were going to a family reunion at a resort about an hour out of our hometown. Maybe we could get together. My letter was long, wanting to catch up on the big pieces of my life these long years later while avoiding sounding too needy or hopeful. I licked the envelope shut and kissed it then popped it in the mailbox. "Hurry, snail mail," I whispered.

I had not been expecting to be in a romantic relationship at this juncture of my life. Motherhood and work took all my time, energy and attention. Best that we become pen pals. Except the dam holding back my love for him was already breaking.

After a week, his next letter (finally) arrived, and I quickly ripped it open. This time he used a couple of pages to tell me about himself. He started out by writing that one day, while out for a walk to the railroad tracks where we used to hang out, joyful memories of our times together started emerging "out of nowhere" that led him to weepy episodes that lasted hours. He said he'd had a hard time hiding the tears at work. When he regained his composure, he decided to send the card with his note.

Those sentimental words were followed by some impersonal details of his life. After he graduated from college, he had moved back to our hometown in Maine, had never married, and had no kids. He was working as a nurse with disabled children. I thought the tone of the rest of the letter sounded a bit guarded, revealing nothing more of his emotions. He said he would be home and wanted to see Lynn again and meet my friend Liam. "Is Liam," he asked, "your partner or husband?"

We started to email each other, but, though I let him know that Liam and I were just good friends, I wasn't ready to tell him I hadn't dated in the five years since Lynn was born. Nor did I tell him that all my romantic interests over the years had been overshadowed by the memory of what I'd had with him. I did make sure he knew I had another love now to nurture and sustain—a mother's love.

Then phone calls to each other started becoming a daily thing. I began wondering how he might fit into the picture that was my current life, but I had to be patient and wait to find out more when we got together.

A couple of weeks before the trip North, I dug out a short storybook illustrated with photos that I had made after Dave and I had said our last goodbyes. A story of unrequited love, a story I had never shared with him since we broke up those many years ago. It had been a way for me to process my loss at the time. Brushing off the dusty cover, I sat down to have another look at it.

SAVE THE GORILLAS

Once upon a time, there was a man named Dave. He was a warm, loving soul. One day, he was sitting by the railroad tracks, contemplating his life, and he met Samantha, who also liked to listen to and watch the trains. They became the best of friends, eventually meeting each other's families, and fell in love.

On some of their dates, Dave would show up dressed as a gorilla, rehearsing for the annual Earth Day and May Day parades.

Several years in a row, Dave and I had participated together in those parades. I would wear a festive colorful dress. While a friend of ours played his accordion, we danced down the streets, passing out flyers that explained the plight of the endangered gorillas of Africa. The accompanying pictures in that story brought back a flood of memories.

Samantha was afraid of gorillas, and even when Dave was out of costume, she was so fearful of his love that one day she ran away. It didn't take her long to realize though that Dave had been the most important person in her life and now he was suddenly gone, by her doing. She felt caught between her yearning to see him and afraid to be vulnerable, but she worked up her courage to call him and ask him to stop by.

Soon after seeing Dave again, she realized she had been resisting love and if she could just give in, it could be as magical as she had always imagined.

When Samantha told Dave she was ready to commit her love to him, his response was cool. He told her he didn't trust her and felt unsafe. He said he was no longer willing to see what would happen to her stubborn stance of not having a family.

Samantha could not commit to that. Dave said he needed space.

At this writing, Samantha is wondering if too much damage has been done and their relationship is irreconcilable. Must she accept that her beloved gorilla is extinct? Should she have faith in the future? Meanwhile, she campaigns in her heart for all other endangered love relationships, praying that they may find ways to find common ground, forgive indecision, learn to trust, and come to know peace. Please join her campaign. Save the Gorillas!

Inside the book I found a copy of the flyer I used to pass out to people standing along the parade route. And there was another flyer written for the story as a parallel campaign that said, "Help Save a Human Gorilla." The organizations one could donate to were: Estranged Gorillas Anonymous, c/o Dave, living on Broken Heart Rd., or Runaway Rehabilitation, Inc. c/o Samantha, living on Lovers Lane.

On the last pages of the story was a reward offered for anyone finding the gorilla. There was a copy of a $100 bill with a gorilla's face covering up Benjamin Franklin's face. When you turned to the final page it said: "The End?"

I put the storybook down, feeling such a glow of warmth in my heart. I could hardly wait to take it with me to Maine to show Dave.

Letting Love Flow

By the time we finally got together, meeting again as more mature adults, we knew things had changed and we were ready for something much deeper. I was a mother now, something I couldn't fathom at the time we were together, something that had been a major barrier to my committing my love to him. His trust in me had now returned.

Standing in the doorway of his cabin nestled in the Maine woods with Liam and Lynn as witnesses to our reunion, I felt like time stood still. Dave and I embraced for the first time in ages. We almost forgot about Lynn and Liam until Lynn at last said, "Ahem, mother. Have you forgotten about us?"

"Lynn, honey, Dave is a very special old friend. Hey, Liam, I want you to meet Dave, too." They shook hands and secretly winked at one another, two six feet tall handsome men: Liam with beautiful Native American features and Dave a brown hair and bearded, trim lumberjack with developed musculature.

"Liam, I know we just got here, but would it be possible for you two to go for a walk, maybe stretch your legs and look around and let us have some time alone? It's been so very long since we saw each other!"

Liam smiled at us and said, "Hey, Lynn, there's a train museum in this town. Let's go get a look at it." Lynn rolled his eyes and then followed Liam out the door, saying as he turned to look at Dave, "You better be nice to my mom." Dave was relieved to see that Liam was truly just a dear friend of ours, an uncle figure to Lynn, deeply connected to one another.

With Lynn and Liam gone, Dave and I entered his home. A bouquet of daisies greeted me on the kitchen table. He had done some research to find out what my favorite flowers were! I was charmed by his sentimental nature. After the six-week period of getting reacquainted from afar, it didn't take long for us to reestablish and reaffirm our love for one another. We both felt we already had a solid foundation from what now seemed like only yesterday.

Liam and Lynn took time later that day to get to know Dave, asking questions about his favorite games, what kind of work he did, what he got excited about in life, and where his family lived. Lynn had never acted jealous of anyone around me before, but suddenly he was clearly being protective of our connection. He became clingy and would not leave my side.

The following day, after our slumber party in Dave's living room (except I had sneaked off in the middle of the night to snuggle with Dave), Liam decided that he and Lynn should clear out and give us some more time alone. It was hard for Lynn to see me kissing Dave. He told us in no uncertain terms that it looked "gross."

After a big pancake breakfast, the two of them set off to check out the cabin we'd reserved, and to spend a few days with family members before the big reunion. Lynn had plenty of cousins around his age to play with, and Liam would be easily welcomed and fit in with my family.

Will You Commit Your Love?

A honeymoon of honeymoons rolled out for us over those next few days, full of the ecstasy you might read about in romance novels. I showed Dave my *Save the Gorillas* book and we reminisced about days gone by until we cried. We marveled at how our deep feelings had survived over such a long time. We shared our mutual inspiration from Rumi translations and the philosophy behind the poetry, how Rumi's poems apply to our human search for the Infinite/God, and how we can sometimes see the infinite in each other. Then, Dave read me one, dedicating it to me to illustrate this:

The minute I heard my first love story I
started looking for you,
not knowing how blind that was.
Lovers don't finally meet somewhere.
They're in each other all along.

Then I read him one of my favorites:

Your task is not to seek for
love, but merely to seek and find
all the barriers within yourself
that you have built against it.

On our last evening alone, we drove into town so we could take a walk along the railroad tracks where we'd met. It was a balmy moonlit night, and a few stars were visible above the city lights. When we arrived at the tracks, I got down on my knees, and put my head to the ground, as if listening for a train. I pretended to discover something surprising on the ground.

"Look, Dave," I said. "I found a treasure!" I held up the diamond ring he had given me fifteen years earlier. He was dumbfounded.

It was my turn now. "Dave, will you commit your love to me?" I proposed. I held the ring up to catch a beam of moonlight then put it on my ring finger and signed, "I love you."

"Samantha, are you serious?" he asked, incredulous.

I nodded my head "Yes," took his hand, and looked into his eyes, and insisted, "Ask me again!"

"Samantha, are you SERIOUS?" he repeated, his brown eyes wide open.

"Yes, Dave," I said. "Yes, yes, YES!"

We were wiping tears of joy on each other's shirts as we heard the familiar whistle announcing the oncoming train. We held each other close as the cars rumbled by, shouting at the top of our lungs, our voices echoing again and again, "I love you! *I love you!*" I can still remember, as clearly as if it had been yesterday, those crazy, joyful moments when our future together became real for us.

Over the years I had used the diamond ring when going to places where I might get hit on by other guys. I wanted to give the message I was taken. Now I could flaunt it in honesty.

Prize Fish

The following morning was a perfect summer day with no rain in the forecast. Both Dave and I were each carrying a warm special glow as we drove to the lake for my big family reunion. Dave knew my family all those years ago, occasionally bumping into my siblings around town, and so he was able to instantly reconnect with them. He was gallant with my mom, and she was eating it up. One of my brothers got him going on fishing stories and we all sat around laughing uproariously.

They never let Dave hear the end about the "prize fish" he'd caught. Everyone teased us two lovebirds. My mother even blurted out, "I wonder if Dave will turn into a snowbird and fly south for the winter?" For the moment we had decided to keep our commitment plans a secret. We felt ready but not ready to tell this crowd about it. I wanted to break the news to them once we'd had more time to figure out the logistics of such a sudden and big change for each of us.

I hadn't spoken to Liam about Dave much since we'd been friends. He assumed that the relationship was "out of sight, out of mind," since Dave hadn't stayed in touch. So, Liam was perplexed by my news. He had never seen me so smitten and took me aside for a talk. He told me he wished, "on some level," that he was the one I loved. But at the same time, he wanted to give me his blessing.

I was a little choked up. To change the serious tone I said, "Liam, if Dave doesn't pick you to be the witness for him, will you be my maid of honor?" We laughed so hard, it got everyone's attention. They were curious about our private conversation, but that was between us.

Before dark, Dave set up a tent for the two of us for the night. It was like reliving our old camping days. Since it was still early in the summer, there were few bugs to deal with other than some pesky mosquitoes.

Meanwhile, a bunch of us were sitting around an open fire cooking up smores. Dave joined up and we all talked late into the evening about the good 'ol' days. We shared lots of stories about working in our big family garden. Lynn and Liam enjoyed listening to the family tales.

Liam told the harrowing story of the time he and Lynn and I were on a boat a mile off the Atlantic coast trolling along as the sun began to set. Suddenly, the motor died. Then the paddle broke. Our hearts sank and we were scared for a bit. Liam's clever solution saved us from our plight that night. He would throw the anchor out and each time it hit bottom, he would reel us in closer to land, finally reaching the dock by dark. The Coast Guard had been looking for us as we pulled up and applauded Liam's ingenuity.

Not Saying Good-Bye This Time

The following day, when Dave headed back to town for work, it was hard to say goodbye. We eased the sadness of parting by vowing to start planning his move south as soon as Lynn and I were back home. A month later, after a nonstop email and phone exchange, both of us still on a lover's high, he drove down to scope out the area and spent several days going to job interviews he'd started setting up from Maine.

He took his time getting to know Lynn. As Lynn continued to warm up to him, Dave said to me that he hoped he would pass muster and win Lynn's trust.

We set things in motion before he left, agreeing to have an informal commitment celebration at the park down by the railroad tracks in our hometown. Dave assured me he would find out the train schedules because we'd decided it would be nice to have those sounds as background harmony during our festivities.

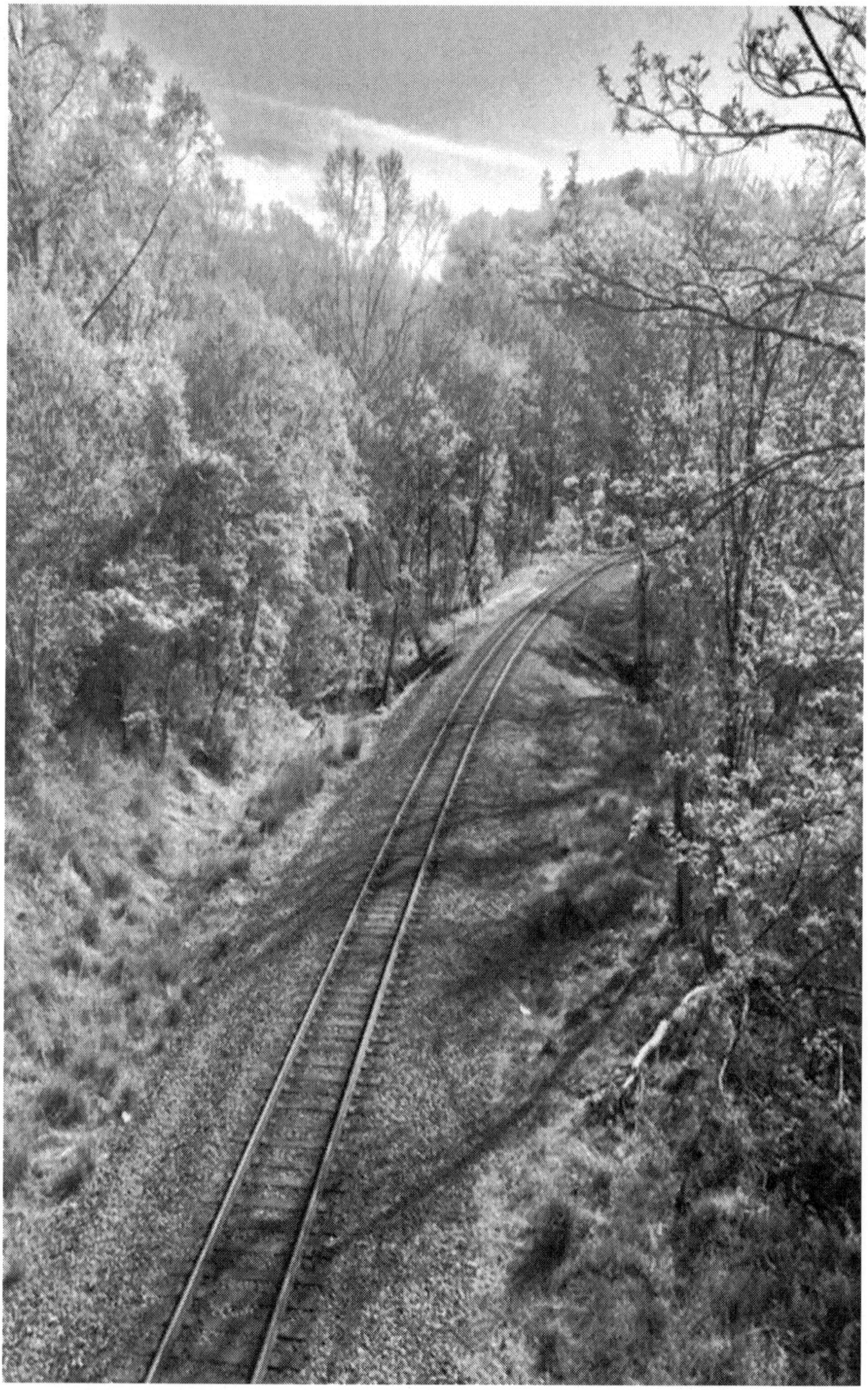

Putting all of the pieces together would take more time. We wanted to be careful not to make any announcement until the right moment, certainly well before the winter winds blew again.

From that time on, with Dave solidly in the picture, my family life became complete. Our bond of love was the centering foundation I'd been searching for, unbeknownst to myself, for a long, long time.

21
Reflections

I OFTEN QUOTE THE PERSON who went through Outward Bound and then famously said, "I wouldn't trade this experience for a million dollars and I wouldn't do it again for two million." It's the kind of wisdom that only makes sense in hindsight. I wonder why we aren't provided with better lenses to begin with.

Looking back to the time when postpartum hell almost wrecked my life *and Lynn's*, I shudder to think how close I came to missing the happiness I found later on. My trial-by-fire led me to a new lease on life. Though I didn't know it at the time, the ordeal actually blessed me with multiple miracles. I have found that the more I believe in miracles, the more I create and work towards opportunities for them to arise, the more they roll out before my eyes, creating a panorama of peace, ease, happiness, and an infinitude of possibilities. I am convinced that this cannot be true for me alone but is possible for all of us.

Most of us have "gorillas" we fear, and we often build walls as protection from the beast. I had arrived at a place where I let down those walls. I could look back at my fears and understand the quote that goes: *"That which we resist, persists."*

I had excelled at being on the run, excited by the beautiful web I'd woven with its diverse relationships, travel opportunities, and inspiring jobs. I've since learned I could still enjoy all this at a slower pace while admitting that life can include what you really long for inside, wherever you are living, if one welcomes it. The belief that I was the luckiest person alive *only* if I were free from commitments had been transformed.

Now I could see that there is no amount of adventure that would let me dodge the pitfalls in life that had brought loneliness, uncertainty, pain and despair. In that place of humility, I finally felt comfortable with the experience of being human in all its manifestations. Deep introspection and reflection had enabled me to see that my habits of staying busy, trying new things, and living on the edge had functioned in part as avoidance mechanisms; they allowed me to skip over the more conventional, ordinary trials of life. I now know that any kind of backdrop to one's life does not exempt them from everyday human suffering.

I had discovered how to surrender to life—to take it all in, even "normal" everyday encounters—without dodging what I used to judge as mundane, and then replacing it with something more exciting. I was finding each day to be so rich. Though it was still full of risks and unavoidable wrong turns, I realized I could make the best of life. And there was room for special kinds of love.

To fill the missing connection in my heart, I could have gotten addicted to drugs; I had certainly experimented and enjoyed highs from psychedelics. I might have become an alcoholic, or a shopaholic, or gotten caught up in some food obsessions. Workaholism did get the best of me at times, though I played hard too. Sometimes when life got too difficult to be myself, suicide had seemed like a tempting alternative.

Motherhood pierced my heart and woke my spirit allowing a Divine Grace to open me fully to Real Love. After Lynn was born, I couldn't run away from him. My maternal instinct, and lucky stars, refused to let me let go of my precious baby.

Playing with fire in the arena of adoption as a birthmother-essentially giving birth to an empty nest—took me to my knees. Though I barely touched the surface of what it means to relinquish a child, it was a frightful alley I went down. The whole experience was enough trauma for a lifetime. Perhaps it was a necessary step, the only thing capable of eventually waking me up to opportunities for a greater, more genuine joy.

I consider this scary close call with relinquishing a child my most challenging life lesson. It was an initiation that opened in me a deep well of compassion for birthmothers, adoptees, and their families, each of whom must also navigate the complexities that follow in the wake of such choices and decisions. We all get huge assignments in life that can make us a better person but not before we walk through fire. As excruciating as I found traveling through the valley of hopelessness and regret to be, I now understand that this journey gave me the greatest blessing on all levels of my life!

With this realization in mind, I say to all those impacted by my choices: "I'm sorry. Please forgive me. Thank you and I love you."

No matter how deeply we've suffered in the past or still suffer today, it truly is possible to find the hidden treasures that can bring us back to our Selves. With even one small seed of faith, a tiny spark of hope, and perseverance, we may experience both renewal and delight. These gifts are revealed through embracing the awesomeness of life rather than resisting its truth.

Gareth Higgens' poem in his book *how not to be afraid*, speaks to this power of embracing all that life has to offer.

A Blessing for Breath

Breathe,
knowing that every molecule
both within and without your body is stardust
and imbued with the light of God—
nothing separate, all a spiral into and from Love.

Breathe,
knowing that the worst pain in your life
has already been experienced by the mercy of the universe.

Breathe,
knowing that if the stones yearn to become cathedrals,
then you—enfleshment of divinity, mingling of sacred and profane,
a little lower than the angels—
are not the sum total of the worst things that have happened to you
or the worst things you have done.

Breathe,
knowing that the ones you admire the most—
the Gandhis and Mother Teresas and Fannie Lou Hammers
and those who clear land mines and lie down with lions for the sake of peace—
these are the fruits of lives that have been crucibled in suffering.

No one becomes great without first being brought low. No one develops true empathy for the greatest suffering without touching some of that suffering themselves.

Breathe. [10]

---

[10] "A Blessing for Breath" by Gareth Higgens, *how not to be afraid* (Broadleaf Books, 2021). Used by permission.

22
Twins!

MY HEART WAS POUNDING as I dialed the number. "Ring-a-ling-a-ling," reverberated through the phone. I was feeling a mixture of excitement and trepidation as I faced talking to my mother. I was determined to put an end to the difficult charades she had witnessed me create throughout my life. Pregnancy conversations had been especially heavy for us in the past—my first pregnancy ended in a miscarriage, my second evolved into an adoption process followed by a revocation, and now my mom was unexpectedly going to be a grandma again!

"Ring-a-ling-a-ling."

"Hello?"

"Hi, Mom, are you sitting down?"

"Samantha?"

"Yes, Mom. I have some big news that I am excited to tell you."

Silence.

"Mom?"

"I am sitting down, and I am listening. Nothing will surprise me."

"Thanks Mom. Okay, ummm… I'm three months pregnant. With twins! And I'm keeping them. I've been meaning to tell you, Mom, really. I'm sorry. Please forgive me for taking so long to call; I just wanted to make sure the pregnancy was going okay. Tell everyone for me, will you?"

"Oh Samantha! Congratulations. I've been hearing some Rumors about Dave. Is he the father?"

"Yes, of course he is Mom!"

"That's wonderful! I hadn't heard much since you were up here together. You know these surprises are making me old before—"

"Stop, Mom, please! I just wanted to give you the good news. Let's talk later, maybe this weekend."

"Okay," she sighed. "Whenever you have more time, Samantha. I love you."

"Thanks, Mom." I replied. "I love you too."

Epilogue

LIFE'S ROLLER COASTER RIDE took me on more spins with happiness and grief. Just when I thought and felt I was finally settled in my life, more tragedy hit. While my twins were young, we lost Dave, and then Liam. There were others who passed. It would require another book to share the tolls that those deaths took, while somehow opening my heart to contain the precious memories that are still alive.

After Dave's death I swore off romantic relationships, only dabbling in a few explorations that included a desire to coparent with a potential stepfather, but those elusive chases always came with red flags. I mostly stayed busy raising Lynn and my twins, somehow fitting in travel adventures, while always embraced by the support of family, friends, and a broader community container. At the core was my commitment and love of motherhood which sustained me. Ralph's help was invaluable while raising Lynn.

As Lynn set out on his own life, in one of our farewell's, I said, "Someday, perhaps when you have children of your own you will understand your mother's love. You are the best thing that ever happened to me."

"I never want to have kids." He said in a determined voice.

"Now wait, that was my line, and I was so wrong! Look at how much I have been blessed with you in my life."

"Whatever mom, gotta go." With a kiss on the cheek, he turned around scurrying off. My eyes welled up with tears as I watched him until he was out of sight. I stood there and wept. The nest would be empty without him.

My mother worried and wondered if I would ever recover from my losses. She wanted me to find someone special. When the twins were 16 my mother's health took a turn for the worse. After a month of hospitalization and rehab. I visited her and my family to see where I could be of help. To honor my mom's wish to be at home I committed to spending half my time living in Maine to help care for her. The twins were mature enough to manage. Lynn and my community network of support helped. My job was portable and flexible so I could take some part-time work. With so many siblings, seven living in my hometown and everyone pitching in, this was manageable.

Caring for my mother was exhausting and, as hard as it is to admit, I burned out three years into this arrangement. The Epstein Barr virus came back to haunt me, and my body was akin to a dead battery. A brother from out of town lovingly stepped in to take my shifts with my mother. "Samantha, I've got this," he said, "for as long as it takes to revive yourself."

My mother blamed herself for my burnout and worried about me. After much self-care, soul-searching, and nourishment from others, I somehow regained a heightened sense of a sweetness and appreciation for life. Then when I wasn't looking, romance beckoned. It had blossomed in the faces of everyone in my life, and then in the form of a caring and loving man named Spencer.

Ironically Spencer had moved into the neighborhood and was renting a room from Angela! He went on walks around the block and often saw me coming and going. One day as I was pulling into my driveway, he was waving his arms like a whirligig to get my attention. It turned out he was motioning me to stop. "I've lost my flash drive and I'm retracing my steps." That opened up our conversation and we exchanged phone numbers. Initially I prefaced my conversations with him letting him know I was not interested in a romance but would consider a friendship. Truth be told, early on I knew I had met someone with whom I felt a strong connection. No amount of rationalizing and resistance could keep me from this man.

Six months into our friendship we both opened up to romance with each other. Spencer and I had planned a trip to the beach when I got a call from my family and learned that my mother had had a bad fall. I called her.

"Ring-a-ling-a-ling."

She answered in a weak voice, "Hello?"

"Mom, how are you, I heard you fell."

"I fell off a ladder."

"Off a ladder?" She was confused. She had fallen off her bed.

"When are you coming home, Samantha?"

"I'll be home this summer, in just a few months."

"Come tomorrow," she insisted.

"Ma, I'll be there this summer, okay?"

"Come tomorrow. I'm a magician."

"OK mom, I'll come. I'll see you soon. I love you."

"I love you too. Bye."

When Spencer arrived that evening to discuss final plans for our beach trip, I said, "My mom had a fall and asked me to come 'tomorrow.' I would feel guilty if something happened to her while we were at the beach. Will you come with me?"

"I don't know your family and I would feel like I'm imposing on a situation where I don't belong. They wouldn't appreciate a stranger being around at a time like this."

"Please Spencer. My mother has been so concerned about me and has wanted me to meet someone special, and I think that's you. I want you to meet her while she is still alive."

Spencer wanted to sleep on it and the next day he said, "Yes. I know this is important. I'll come."

I hugged him tight. I let myself be supported instead of saying, "I can do this myself and I don't need anyone." This was going to be an important passage.

Enroute to Maine, at the top of a mountain pass, as a form of prayer, we stopped and lit sage and smudged ourselves. Then we called in the four directions as a blessing for the journey ahead.

When we arrived, a few sisters were at my mother's side with hospice backing them up. She looked so beautiful, like she had just come from the hair salon. She was covered with a soft pink blanket and seemed relaxed. The morphine medication was at work, giving her relief from pain and slowly helping her release her body to the great beyond. She had known I was coming, and she had waited. My heart was bursting with love.

I looked in her eyes, and she mine. Her face lit up with a big smile. "Hi mom. I'm home!" I said softly and slowly, while feeling an urgency to say what I had to say. "I want you to know I am doing well, and you can stop worrying about me. You can go. I will miss you and I love you, and mom, remember you wanted me to meet someone special?"

She stared at me, not uttering a word.

"I brought him with me. Mom, this is Spencer." I pointed at him, and she moved her head slowly to look at him, then back at me, then at him, all the while smiling.

She struggled to get her words out, then said: "Very nice," then she whispered, "Yeah." Those were her last words ever. She passed away a week later.

The sadness is something still fresh. Grief is working its way through the pipeline of my family.

Life is still full of surprises. I am grateful that my mother got to meet Spencer. Several months after the magic of those last words spoken by my mother, on a full blue moon, we went for a hike at a wooded park near the river where we first held hands. I was scared as I proposed to him, committing my love to him, asking if he would be willing to commit to me in the form of a "handfast" ritual in the not-too-distant future—the kind of ritual where we would make a promise to stay together for a year to begin with. "If you will, would you place my mother's wedding ring on my finger? She asked me to save it for a special moment with a special someone." I believed she was here with us using her magic to create such a miracle.

He placed my mother's wedding ring on my finger. Without words he looked at me lovingly and held me, shaking his head, "Yes."

Love is in the air, it is everywhere. We feel it in our children, in our family, in our friendships, in our romantic partnership, and in nature. May those ripples extend out to embrace the whole world. In the end it is love that prevails.

We are living happily ever after.

Acknowledgments

CONTINUING WITH THE THREAD of honoring confidentiality, I am acknowledging my connections with people by including fictitious names. The following points to some of the more recent players on the forefront of my journey, not to diminish any of you who have touched my life. I have so many people to thank for our ongoing sharing of discovery and connection.

My dedication to my son, Lynn, and my twins, is filled with gratitude for them being in this world, allowing me to experience a wider range love, from the deepest joy I have ever known, to that of patience through navigating life's challenges; I aspire to have this unconditional joy and tolerance with everyone, whether or not we are kin. The world awaits it.

This initiation of motherhood wove a strong web. Ralph, I thank you for joining me on a wild ride into the unknown territory of adoption, revocation, and parenthood, traversing dark corners, and coming through many tests with greater compassion and wisdom.

To all the inspirations for the characters in this story, I thank you from the bottom of my heart for gracing my life with your friendship and love.

To midwives, birthmothers, adoptees, and adoptive families for paving the way to new understandings. You continue to teach me about the complexity of navigating this journey.

Nancy Verrier, consultation with you changed my life. Your personal experience as a parent of both a biological and an adopted child, and the books you wrote from the knowledge you gained in your work with clients that are players in the adoption triangle, informed me at a critical juncture. I am forever grateful.

I will never forget you, my ancestors, as you assist me from the ethers. This includes my parents, two of my brothers (Earl & Anthony), extended family members who have passed on, the Manning grandparents, the Lynnwood grandparents, dear friends: Sammy, and Liam, and there are so many others. I am saddened by your final departures. We've got to talk.

Thanks to my beloved siblings and my extended family, including all the layers of aunts, uncles, cousins, in-laws, nieces, nephews, and treasured homeland and lifetime friends, my witnesses and audience, often aghast by my inability to follow conventional and conditioned rules—and there to help me pick up the pieces when I fall.

Thank you to my rural ecovillage founders and collaborators, some I call my dream weavers: Peter, Keith and Chaz; some of my PALs: Pab, Alden, Larry; the Kim sisters: Kim, Sue, and Patricia; those sharing sacred land and support with Lynn's entry; and furthermore all those who have contributed with hands and hearts on the ecovillage project, including those who continue carrying the commitment and exemplary work towards building sustainable lifestyles that seek to serve this and future generations.

To counselors and healers, for providing guidance through steep learning curves, especially Bonita, Emma, Jay, and Sheila.

To the Deaf community, for teaching me your language and culture, giving me both deep friendships and a career that allowed flexibility to navigate life's juggling act. I've had the best job in the world! Especially thanks to Cindy, Linda, John, and Clarence, for planting the seeds for my career.

Antonio Meucci (of Italy), thank you for your work on inventing the telephone, my lifeline in my darkest hours.

Ruth, I appreciate you encouraging me to write down the story!

I thank my editing coaches: Arjuna and Kiesa. Arjuna, you witnessed and then held my hand in documenting this ride. We have shared home, hearth, and healthy food. You have showered me with deep insights, most recently bringing clarity to this story while massaging the edits. Kiesa, thanks for giving me support and direction, asking me questions: "What do you see, smell, and hear? How do you feel? Show, don't tell." Then applauding my milestones.

Dana, you dropped out of the sky in the 11th hour, suggesting another layer of editing, enhancing what I had thought was the final product. I was tired, but you reinspired me, which carried the book to its final iteration, using your expertise in making it much more readable. I am so grateful!

Thank you to those who read the draft in its various forms and gave me more pointers: Amana, David, Penny, Paul, Vanna, Beth, Grace, Carol, Seraina, Carole, and Jo. And thanks to my housemates who gave me space to be reclusive, including Jon who often shared his leftovers and Marcia who fed me Macrobiotic meals.

To those who shared inspirational quotes and poetry, including Rumi translators; for the versions in this book, Coleman Barks, I thank you. I want to kiss your feet. Shanti Rose, I appreciate your ongoing collaboration in creating a unique collection of these gems that continue to serve, inspire, and guide me. Besides that, our long friendship fills my heart with gladness. Spencer, thanks for sharing the songs and their lyrics that move your soul, and then they become infectious in me. ILYSMMTYCEPIBYWDTIAB.

Ramajon, thanks for your invaluable guidance in the initial book and cover design. Formatting required more edits than what you signed up for! I appreciate your patience with all the details and delays. Pepi, you started adding final brushstrokes, then I had you paint the whole house! This included creating the final cover design. You saw from first glance where typographic assistance was needed; there were so many "orphans" and "widows," new terms to me. They needed to be rescued so you jumped on board. Levi, thanks for was letting me borrow your daddio. He is so dedicated to you, and you were gracious in celebrating what he was accomplishing.

To you, the readers, I am honored to have had your time. We grow through connection. We are walking one another home. It has been a delight to share a story from my heart to yours.

To all those friends and family members who caught me in the times I fell and helped me get back on my feet. I like to think I have 9 lives, but not without the loving support I have received.

To the little girl inside, who grew up and took the world by storm, finding her way to her birthright of wholeness.

Finally, to a loving God, who weeps and laughs behind the scenes.

My Inspiration

Books

Aldo, Joseph. *In an Ecstatic State, Poems of Transformation*

Allen, Rajyo. *Fumbling Towards Freedom, Initiation on the Path of Awakening*

Almaas, A. H. *The Diamond Approach*

Bailey, Alice A. *Ponder on This*

Bane, Peter. *The Permaculture Handbook*

Barks, Coleman. *Essential Rumi: New Expanded Version Harper,* and *The Illuminated Rumi*

Biddle MD, James. *Reclaim Your Health, An Integrative Medicine Pathway*

Blanton PhD, Brad. *Practicing Radical Honesty*

Brach PhD, Tara. *Radical Acceptance, Embracing Your Life with the Heart of a Buddha*

Braden, Gregg. *The God Code*

Combs, Sharon B. *Healthy Nutrition, Your Easy-To-Follow Guide for a Healthy Diet*

Desai, Penache. *You Are Enough*

Dr. David Chamberlain. *Babies Remember Birth*

Dispenza, Dr. Joe. *Breaking the Habit of Being Yourself*

Dufty, William. *Sugar Blues*

Eisenstein, Charles. *Sacred Economics, Money, Gift, and Society in the Age of Transition*

Gates, Donna. *The Body Ecology Diet: Recovering Your Health and Rebuilding Your Immunity*

Gibran, Kahlil. *The Prophet*

Goldberg, Burton. *Alternative Medicine, the Definitive Guide*

Hausner, Stephan. *Even if it Costs Me My Life, Systemic Constellations and Serious Illness*

Haas MD, Elson M. *Staying Healthy with Nutrition, The Complete Guide to Diet and Nutritional Medicine*

Higgins, Gareth. *How Not to be Afraid*

Jacobson, Leonard. *Embracing the Present, Bridging Heaven and Earth, Words from Silence, Journey into Now, In Search of the Light,* and *Liberating Jesus*

Jensen, Derrick. *A Language Older Than Words*

Kellman MD, Raphael. *The Microbiome Diet*

Lamp, Linda. *Walking Through Your Walls*

Levine, Peter. *Waking the Tiger*

Lipton PhD, Bruce. *The Biology of Belief*

Lolling, Lila. *Walking the Ancient Path of Yoga*

Mate MD, Gabor. *The Myth of Normal, Trauma, Illness, and Healing in a Toxic Culture*

Moore, Thomas. *Care of the Soul*

O'Brien. *Christianity and Yoga*

O'Donohue, John. *Anam Cara: A Book of Celtic Wisdom*

Pitchford, Paul. *Healing with Whole Foods, Asian Traditions and Modern Nutrition*

Pollan, Michael. *How to Change Your Mind*

Pueblo, Yung. *Clarity and Connection*

Robbins, Tom. *Even Cowgirls Get the Blues*

Schmidt, Tracy. *I have fallen in love with the world*

Schucman, Helen. *A Course in Miracles*

Shaw, Darwin C. *Effort and Grace*

Shroyer, Whitney, and Letitia Walker. *Sock Monkey Dreams*

Singer, Michael A. *the untethered soul*

Soll, Joe. *Adoption Healing…a path to recovery*

Song, Tamarack. *Truthspeaking Ancestral Ways to Hear and Speak the Voice of the Earth*

Safransky, Sy. *Sunbeams A Book of Quotations*

Smartt, Lisa. *Words at the Threshold, What We Say as We're Nearing Death*

Stanchich, Leno. *Power Eating Program, You Are How You Eat*

Styron, William. *Darkness Visible*

Tolle, Eckhart. *A New Earth Awakening to Your Life's Purpose*

Verrier, Nancy Newton. *The Primal Wound: Understanding the Adopted Child* and *Coming Home to Self: The Adopted Child Grows Up*

Yogananda, Paramahansa. *Man's Eternal Quest*

Wilbur, Ken. *A Brief History of Everything*

Zinn, Howard. *A People's History of the United States*

Movies

And Your Name is Jonah
August Rush
The Bird Cage
Children of a Lesser God
CODA
The Danish Girl
Hugo
Lion
Philomena
Untamed Heart
Wild Life

Websites

danny-carroll.com
ecovillage.org
ic.org
localharvest.org/csa
loveandlogic.com
onewhowakes.org
reckoningwiththeprimalwound.com
wwoof.net

About the Author

SAMANTHA SONG IS BOTH a fictional character and a pen name. The invented characters represent overlapping circles of fiction and circles of truth. Those circles remind me how in the Flower of Life design one circle flows into the next culminating in a beautiful design full of magical connections.

I first discovered the Flower of Life design in a junior high school art class by doodling circles with a compass. What emerged excited me. My art teacher encouraged me to paint it on an 8 x 8 foot canvas using primary colors at the center that became secondary and tertiary colors as the design moved outward. The canvas was displayed on a wall I passed daily. Its appearance had a kaleidoscopic effect that always filled me with delight. Years later, I learned of its meaning.[11] To me, this symbol represents the great web of life and furthermore how our stories overlap and connect us.

Now it's your turn to share your colorful story. Thank you for your precious time in reading mine.

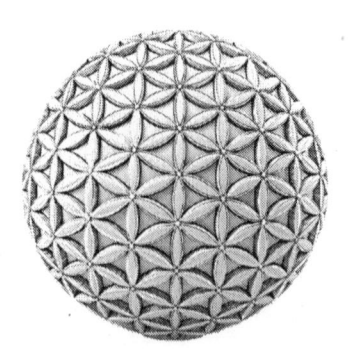

Spencer Elbert, artist

---

[11] See *uniguide.com/flower-of-life-sacred-geometry* for more information on the Flower of Life.